P9-BJC-613

WIN THE RIGHT WAY

WIN THE RIGHT WAY
How to Run Effective
Local Campaigns in California

Christine Trost and Matt Grossmann, editors

Berkeley Public Policy Press
Institute of Governmental Studies
Berkeley, California
2005

© 2005 by the Regents of the University of California. All rights reserved.

Library of Congress Cataloging-in-Publication Data

Win the right way : how to run effective local campaigns in California / edited by
Christine Trost and Matt Grossmann.
    p. cm.
  ISBN 0-87772-417-2
  1. Local elections--California. 2. Campaign management--California. I. Trost, Christine. II. Grossmann, Matthew.

JS451.C25W56 2005
324.7'09794--dc22   2004030124

This guide represents a collaborative effort between The Center for Campaign Leadership and the Institute for Local Self Government. CCL (campaigns.berkeley.edu) is a nonpartisan, campaign training and research organization located at UC Berkeley's Institute of Governmental Studies and is funded by a generous grant from The Pew Charitable Trusts. CCL's mission is to teach practical campaign skills to young people interested in public service and to improve the campaign behavior of candidates and their advisors in a way that encourages greater confidence and participation in American elections and government.

The Institute for Local Self Government (www.ilsg.org) is the nonprofit research arm of the League of California Cities. Its mission is to serve as a forward-thinking source of research and information for California's local officials. A key focus of the Institute's efforts is promoting public confidence in local government and those who serve in local government.

Contents

Preface

Majorities of Americans believe that "negative, attack-oriented campaigning is undermining and damaging our democracy" (82%), that "there is too much money spent on today's campaigns" (86%), that unethical practices in campaigns occur "very" or "fairly" often (58%), and that "in terms of ethics and values, election campaigns in this country have gotten worse in the last 20 years" (53%).[1]

In an effort to improve the state of campaigns in the United States, The Pew Charitable Trusts awarded the Center for Campaign Leadership at the University of California's Institute of Governmental Studies a generous grant to study elite and public opinion about political campaign practices; identify strategies and tactics aimed at encouraging voter participation in campaigns and elections without creating a competitive disadvantage for the candidate; and develop a series of campaign training seminars that teach these "best practices" to candidates and aspiring political consultants.

From March 2002 through October 2003 the Center for Campaign Leadership offered campaign training seminars in different regions of the country to young professionals who were planning to run for office or interested in pursuing a career in campaign politics. The training consisted of four sessions dedicated to the key elements of a winning campaign —message development, message delivery, campaign fundraising, and grassroots mobilization—and panels on ethical and effective campaign practices, media coverage of political campaigns, and the profession of political consulting.

This book seeks to capture and convey the lessons of the research and training that we have conducted over the past three years and share these with a wider audience.

The research presented in this book is based upon findings drawn from a telephone survey of 2000 adult California residents and a series of

---

[1] These figures come from a November 1999 survey conducted by Lake Snell Perry & Associates for The Pew Charitable Trusts and the Institute for Global Ethics, and from a September 2000 survey conducted by Yankelovich Partners, Inc. for the Center for Congressional and Presidential Studies at American University.

focus groups. In the fall of 2002, we worked with the Public Policy Institute of California to design a survey that would assess voters' attitudes about political campaigns in general and, more specifically, towards best practices in campaigns. The survey was conducted in the final eight days leading up to the 2002 gubernatorial election (October 28–November 4) and included interviews in both Spanish and English.

We also designed and conducted six focus groups in three different regions of the state (Walnut Creek, Fresno, and Los Angeles). Each two-hour focus group session had nine to thirteen participants who were diverse with respect to education, income, ethnicity, and party identification. The purpose of the focus groups was twofold: to aid in the design of the statewide survey of California residents, and to provide a closer look at both the range of opinions and beliefs surrounding political campaigns in the United States and California and the processes of evaluation, judgment, and attitude formation that contribute to shaping these opinions and beliefs.

Many hands have contributed to the ideas and advice included in this book, and we wish to acknowledge all of them, beginning with The Pew Charitable Trusts; without its financial support, this book would not have been possible.

We extend our thanks to Dan Schnur, who authored the grant proposal, provided valuable guidance in the development of the statewide survey, led the training seminars, and is codirector of the Center for Campaign Leadership; to Darry Sragow, who was a regular speaker at our training seminars and is codirector of the Center for Campaign Leadership; and to Bruce E. Cain, Robson Professor of Political Science and director of the Institute of Governmental Studies at UC Berkeley, who also served as the principal investigator of the research project. We thank JoAnne Speers, executive director of the Institute for Local Self Government, who is our partner in the publication and distribution of this book and author of "Campaigning Effectively for Local Office: Good People Can Finish First," which we relied on heavily when writing portions of the book. Any success that we may claim in capturing the fruits of our research and the lessons of our training in the pages of this book is due to the leadership and insight that these individuals provided.

Although this guide provides an overview of the relevant law, it is not intended to be legal advice, and it cannot substitute for legal counsel. Also, this guide describes various campaign and election laws, but for brevity's sake, it is not comprehensive and it does not cover every detail and nuance. In short, it should be used as a guide only.

Much of the advice included in this book is drawn from presentations made at the training seminars. We thank the dozens of political consultants who generously shared their time and expertise with our students. We also thank Julia Mitchell and Suneeti Shah, who helped recruit our speakers and students, coordinated the training seminars, and, along with Marc Levin, assistant director of the Institute of Governmental Studies, oversaw the smooth operation of the administrative aspects of the program.

We are especially grateful to Joanne Davis, Mitchell Englander, Jarryd Gonzales, Mary Hughes, Michelle Maravich, Phil Paule, Dan Schnur, Bob Wickers, and Jonathan Wilcox, who, in addition to serving as speakers at our training seminars, wrote essays for this book. JoAnne Speers, Mary Hughes, Dan Schnur, and Bob Wickers also reviewed chapters of the book and provided helpful suggestions for improvements.

We thank Polly Armstrong, Katie Burke, Valerie Hyman and Shaun R. Lumachi for their essays, which add to this book the perspectives of other actors who are involved in political campaigns (candidates, volunteers, donors, and journalists). We are especially grateful to Karen Getman for writing Chapter 8 on the legalities of running for office, and to James Harrison, of Remcho, Johansen & Purcell, for reviewing the entire manuscript to ensure its legal accuracy. We also thank Jerry Lubenow and Maria Wolf, who prepared the book for publication, and Eden James, who proofread the manuscript on a moment's notice.

Finally, Keena Lipsitz and John Sides were vital members of the research team. Together we designed and analyzed the statewide survey of 2000 California residents and designed and conducted the focus groups of California voters. We feel fortunate to have worked with such gifted scholars, and we share equal credit with them for the research findings presented in this book. We also thank Mark Baldassare, Jon Cohen, Lisa Cole, and Dorie Appollonio of the Public Policy Institute of California, who helped design the statewide survey and were responsible for its implementation. Jon Cohen and Lisa Cole also helped conduct several of the focus groups.

Christine Trost
Matt Grossmann

Introduction and Overview

1

Conventional wisdom suggests that candidates for local office must sacrifice their principles to win elections. The only way to win, the story goes, is to skirt the issues and concentrate instead on delivering the lowest blows to your opponents. This perception of what it takes to win turns potential candidates away from running for office and turns potential voters away from the polls. Fortunately, unethical campaign practices do not guarantee victory. Instead, they breed dissatisfied voters and disreputable candidates.

Winning candidates combine ethical campaign practices with effective planning, skillful organizing, and a clear message. They learn about the concerns of their community, the nuts and bolts of organizing, and the intricate rules of financing. They know that campaigning is not easy and they work hard to demonstrate their skills and deliver their message to voters. In doing so, they prove that there is no substitute for careful consideration of local issues, patient coalition building, and painstaking efforts to mobilize supporters.

This book gives you the tools you need to build an effective campaign—without forsaking your values and principles. It is based on new research conducted by both the Center for Campaign Leadership at the University of California, Berkeley, and the Institute for Global Ethics on the concerns of voters. The research shows that voters yearn for candidates who campaign truthfully and fairly, as well as candidates who eschew the dishonest attack-style campaigning that sometimes can seem too prevalent in elections today. The guide also includes advice from leading professionals in every field of campaign strategy and observations from those with experience on local campaigns. Rather than perpetuate the conventional wisdom that negative campaigning is the way to win, this guide shows you how to win *the right way* by adopting tested strategies that allow you to run for office with your principles intact.

What Is an Ethical Campaign?

There are several important elements of an ethical and effective campaign. As a candidate you should ask voters to support you based on your plans to address the issues facing your community. You should treat your fellow candidates with fairness and respect, and avoid personal attacks or mischaracterizations of their positions. Being honest about your views and the kinds of decisions you will make when in office will help, rather than hurt, your chances of election. Using campaign methods that meaningfully engage the public in debate about local policy issues will appeal to voters, encourage them to participate, and help restore their faith in our elections and government.

Ethical campaigning includes more than candidate conduct, however. Unethical campaign strategies can arise from third party mailings and whispering campaigns. Ethical campaigners disavow these inappropriate messages, surround themselves with individuals who do the same, and are vigorous about setting an example for proper behavior on the campaign trail.

Half of the battle is won by creating an environment in which ethical campaigning is expected. You can do this by making your expectations known to your supporters, the media, and your fellow candidates. Set up a series of candidate forums that set the tone for an ethical campaign and encourage follow-up conversations with the media about whether the candidates did indeed walk the talk. Encourage local organizations and voters to hold candidates accountable for abiding by their commitment to conduct ethical campaigns.

Why Should Candidates Be Concerned with Ethics?

There are several reasons candidates should adopt ethical campaign strategies. First, ethical campaign practices can help candidates win elections. It is not necessary to choose between winning and waging an ethical campaign. Professionals have developed a series of best practices for campaigns (presented throughout this guide) that are both ethical and effective. Second, studies show that unethical campaign techniques run a significant risk of backfiring against the candidate who uses them. Even when some unethical tactics may seem to provide political advantage, these unsavory strategies also have the potential to backfire more than others. Third, in most elections voters have little information about the candidates' qualifications or issue stances. The way candidates campaign can send an important signal about how they will govern, which voters can refer to when casting their vote.

Thinking about the Long-Term Consequences of Campaign Strategies

When considering which campaign strategies to adopt, candidates are wise to think about their campaign within the context of their broader political goals. First, political reputations are built over time. Many successful political leaders, including the last three presidents, lose the first time they run for office. It may take longer than one campaign for voters to get to know you. The reputation that you develop, as a good campaigner or as a nasty one, will stick with you—and reputation is everything in local politics. Even if you win, the reputation that you developed in your last campaign can affect how voters perceive you in your next race.

Second, ethical campaigning protects your ability to govern successfully. When you get into office, it is likely that you will need more than your supporters to enact the policies you favor. If you develop a reputation as an ethical politician, even among your political opponents, you will be better prepared to build coalitions in office.

Third, ethical campaigning contributes to increasing voter participation and support for government. Messages that denigrate government and those who serve in government reinforce negative public perceptions about government—perceptions that do not disappear once a candidate leaves the campaign trail and enters public office. Conversely, campaign strategies that engage the public in meaningful debate and dialogue about community issues can help to create more informed citizens and restore the public's trust in democratic government.

Organization of This Guide and Chapter Summaries

This guide contains information on all of the major aspects of running a successful campaign. Here is a chapter-by-chapter breakdown of its contents:

Chapter 1: Before the Campaign

Your campaign should not be the start of your political involvement in the local community. Before you run, learn more about the issues and concerns of your community, the demands of the office that you are interested in seeking, and what it will take to wage a successful campaign. This chapter shows you how.

Chapter 2: Planning Your Campaign

Successful campaigns are well planned from the beginning. Rather than make important decisions as they arise in the campaign, you will need to build a winning strategy and then devote your energies to implementing it. This chapter provides instruction on how to develop your plan of action.

Chapter 3: Building Your Campaign Organization

A candidate cannot win without the help of others. This chapter shows you how to build a solid campaign organization. It covers identifying and recruiting volunteers, hiring paid staff, and building coalitions with other organizations.

Chapter 4: Developing Your Message

Candidates must give voters a reason to vote for them. This chapter explains the components of a winning campaign message. It shows you how to formalize your rationale, develop a convincing theme, and incorporate your issue positions into a message that differentiates your candidacy from others.

Chapter 5: Funding Your Campaign

Running for office requires resources. This chapter tells you what you need to know about developing a fundraising plan, identifying donors, and asking for money. It outlines basic steps involved in raising money for political campaigns and provides practical suggestions for getting your fundraising off the ground.

Chapter 6: Delivering Your Message

Voters will not be persuaded by a message that they never hear. To inform voters and convince them that you should be elected, you will need to use a variety of free and paid media. This chapter outlines the most effective ways to get your message out, including how to speak to the media, how to use advertising and direct mail effectively, and how to set up live opportunities to talk to groups of voters.

Chapter 7: Contacting and Mobilizing Voters

Successful candidates for local office must make direct contact with voters. This chapter shows you how to identify your target populations, contact them by phone and door-to-door canvassing, and develop a get-out-the-vote plan that will get your voters to the polls on Election Day.

Chapter 8: Complying with the Law

Winning elections requires that you avoid illegalities that can sink your campaign. Campaign laws have a number of traps for the unwary and, as a candidate, you will need to learn how to avoid them. This chapter, written by Karen Getman, of counsel to Remcho, Johansen & Purcell and former Chairman of California's Fair Political Practices Commission, shows you how.

Chapter 9: Conclusion—Winning the Right Way

This chapter provides key points for you to review before you start and offers some final thoughts on the challenges and rewards of taking the "high road" to public office.

The Special Features of this Guide

What makes this guide unique is the combination of academic research on what voters want, advice from leading campaign consultants, and descriptions of field-tested strategies from those who have experienced local campaigns. You can expect to see these special features throughout the guide:

Advice from Professionals

We have solicited advice on a range of topics from a distinguished group of California-based professional campaign consultants. Our contributors are respected strategists who help candidates win elections at all levels of government across the state and nation. In their essays, they offer insights gleaned from years of experience working on campaigns, giving readers the benefit of professional advice without paying thousands of dollars in consulting fees.

Advice from the Front Lines

In these sections, you can read about what campaigns are like from those who have spent time on the "front lines." A candidate talks about what it takes to win a local election, a reporter offers tips on how to prepare for interviews with local media, a volunteer describes her reasons for joining a campaign, and a first-time donor explains what motivated him to give to a local candidate.

What Do Voters Want?

This feature highlights what voters want from political candidates and campaigns. It summarizes the results of our statewide survey of 2,000 California residents and in-person focus groups with California voters, in addition to other surveys of voters. We translate the results, giving you recommendations for how to run an effective campaign that will respond to the concerns of voters.

Best Practices and Bright Ideas

In addition to a broad overview of campaigns, we have included specific suggestions for ethical and effective campaign practices in the form of "Best Practices." We also share some specific "Bright Ideas" for implementing the strategies we recommend.

Learn More on the Web

We could not fit all the information that you might need in this book. Throughout the guide, we point you to our Web site (campaigns.berkeley. edu) for more in-depth information, including worksheets, links to important Web sites, campaign calendars, and tips for following the specific laws that apply to campaigns in your area.

Resources for Further Reading

The goal of this guide is to provide candidates for local office with an overview of the elements of a campaign, rather than a complete step-by-step campaign plan. For some campaigns, candidates will want more detail on one or more of these topics. We include "Resources for Further Reading" at the end of the guide to meet this need.

In 1975, California's Institute for Local Self Government published a manual on running for local office: The then-executive director of the Institute observed:

> More importantly, the Institute shares the concern of many Americans over the mounting distrust and disgust with "politicians." We, too, are shaken at the prospect of public disinterest [in politics] because of the failings of a few...Local government is the base upon which this great republic was built and from which it continues to draw its leadership.[1]

The need for strong local leadership provided by people of integrity and principle is no less imperative some thirty years later. This guide is intended to assist you in fulfilling this role. Good luck with your campaign!

---

[1] Bob Norris and Ken Rowe, *How to Take Over Your Local Government*, (Institute for Local Self Government, 1975), vii-viii.

Before the Campaign

1

By the time the campaign starts, some candidates will already have a significant advantage. Candidates with high name recognition among voters, especially those who have developed a reputation as a leader in the community, are much more likely to be elected. You can work hard to improve your image during the campaign, but laying the groundwork in advance will make your task much easier. Take the time to get involved, informed, and well known in your community before the campaign begins; it will pay valuable dividends once you decide to run.

Candidates who become involved in local politics before the campaign have several advantages.

1. They can develop relationships with local leaders, including political party central committee members, community and civic group directors, and local public officials and ask for their endorsements.

2. They may be able to discourage challengers by establishing themselves as the clear front-runner for an office.

3. They can acquire knowledge and experience that will prepare them to discuss local issues and work with local government.

4. They can develop important contacts and supporters who are likely to offer help once the campaign is underway. Experience shows that people are more likely to offer help, including organizational and financial support, if they have a relationship with the candidate before the campaign.

Learning about the Needs and Concerns of Your Constituency

To successfully campaign for local office, you will need to convince voters that you are prepared to address their concerns and that you have the skills, knowledge, and experience to be an effective advocate for their interests. There are many ways to become familiar with the workings of local government so you are prepared when the campaign begins.

- Keep up with local news, controversies, and concerns.

Be on the lookout for any reports of local problems and proposals for possible solutions. Read editorials and letters to the editor in the local papers, listen to local talk radio, and attend local political meetings. When controversies arise over local issues, pay attention to the different policy solutions proposed by local leaders, including their costs and benefits, and their supporters and opponents.

- Get involved with local governance.

Attend meetings of the school board, the city council, the county board of supervisors, and local government agencies like the city planning and zoning commissions. In most cities, there are opportunities to participate on advisory panels or citizen review boards. Make it known that you would like to contribute to local decision making through these venues.

- Join community organizations.

Civic groups such as the League of Women's Voters, the Kiwanis Club, and Rotary International provide opportunities to network with active, local community members. Helping with local charities can connect you to local problems and concerned individuals. Boards of local charities like the United Way provide experience with fundraising and connections with local benefactors. Neighborhood and religious associations can offer early leadership positions and committee responsibilities. Participation in organizations like the Chamber of Commerce and local unions can build ties for future organizing. Local ideological, partisan, and single-issue groups provide opportunities to learn and practice social advocacy.

- Talk with civic leaders.

Before deciding to run for local office, make sure you get a broad sense of the problems and debates in your community by talking to a diverse group of stakeholders. These might include local government administrators, teachers, police officers, religious leaders, developers, businesspeople, activists, and union leaders. Build contacts with people who are knowledgeable in the local policy areas that you think are important.

- ## Learn about the concerns of voters.

Meet with representative groups of local voters. Regularly talk about local issues with people of different ethnic and religious backgrounds, people from different neighborhoods and age groups, and people with different political opinions. It is always better to know the range of opinions in your community.

Learning about the Demands of the Office

Before you run for office, be sure that you truly want to win. Read the description of the office you are seeking and review the history of those who have held the office before you. Talk with current and former office holders and their staffs about the responsibilities and demands of the job. Attend relevant meetings, read news articles, and talk to public officials in offices that work with the one you are interested in assuming.

> ■ **BRIGHT IDEA: Identify Opportunities to Organize Coalitions**
>
> Coalitions can be valuable sources of volunteers and financial support for your campaign. Consider approaching neighborhood associations, nonprofit advocacy groups, local businesses, church groups, labor groups, and service clubs with a request to support your candidacy. Form coalitions around issues that are central to your campaign, such as development (people interested in environmental or planning issues), crime (parents, business owners, youth organizations), or any other key local issue. You can also build coalitions regionally (by neighborhood) or by trade and profession.

Learning about What It Takes to Win

Putting your name before the voters as a candidate for local office is a worthwhile endeavor that contributes to the success of democracy—but it is not an easy task. If you are thinking of running, make sure you know what you are getting into. The first thing to remember is that most candidates lose in any given election. Even those who win usually make large sacrifices to succeed. Here are some of the requirements:

- ## Time and Effort

Running for office requires a significant amount of time and effort. Campaigning will take time away from your family, your work, and your social life. You will enjoy many parts of the campaign, but others may seem tedious (though necessary) and time-consuming.

• Money

Most people who run for office use at least some of their own money to campaign. Some candidates even acquire significant debt in an effort to win. One immediate expense is the cost of not working or working less during the campaign. Even if you do not use your own money, remember that asking for donations can be difficult. It takes persistence and a willingness to ask friends for money.

• Organization

Successful campaigns involve lots of people. You will need the help of many volunteers to get your message out and mobilize voters. As a candidate, you will be the leader of an organization for which you are legally responsible. You will have to rely on others and guide their activities, keep track of details, and respond to the concerns of many people.

• Skills

Being a candidate requires skills that may be different from those required for success in public governance or private life. Good campaigners can apply their skills to the different demands of the campaign, including public relations, financial and personnel management, research, and communication.

• A Thick Skin

As a candidate, you should expect to be asked about things you might consider private, including your education and employment history, business contacts, financial dealings, and family life. Your opponent(s) may say negative things about you. The scrutiny that candidates are frequently subjected to is unavoidable. To withstand the rigors of campaigning, you will need to develop a thick skin.

Do not let this list deter you from pursuing your goal of elected office. Instead, be aware of the demands involved in running for office, weigh them accordingly when you decide to run, and prepare to deal with them when they arise.

Assessing Your Strengths and Weaknesses

Every public official has strengths and weaknesses. Before you become a candidate, assess your strengths and weaknesses both as a candidate and as an officeholder. Think about how others perceive you and how they might respond to your candidacy. Start by asking yourself what your friends like and dislike about you. Then think about any positive or negative comments that strangers sometimes make about you and how they might be relevant in the political arena.

When assessing your strengths, think about your political, interpersonal, and work-related skills, your background and experience, and any areas of expertise that you have developed that can be related to the office that you are seeking. How might your past experiences help you to be a strong candidate or officeholder? Think broadly and remember that being an effective public official requires a diverse set of skills. You should assess your strengths for your own benefit, so that you can rely upon them while you campaign, but also think about how you might describe them to others.

It is even more important to know your weaknesses. Everyone has weaknesses. Make sure that you are aware of yours so that you can address them before and, if necessary, during the campaign. If you lack experience or skills in particular areas that you will need to draw upon during the campaign, try to gain experience in these areas or develop new skills before the campaign begins. Identify other strengths that might allow you to work around your weaknesses. Think of ways to answer criticisms that might be raised about your weaknesses, and how you might recast them as strengths.

Deciding Whether or Not to Run for Office

After you have finished determining what is involved in running for office and assessing your strengths and weaknesses, take time to decide whether or not to run for office. Talk to everyone you trust about your decision and make sure you get a diverse range of views. Remember that your candidacy will impact your family, business associates, and friends; make sure you get the opinions of anyone who might be adversely affected.

Try to accurately assess the challenges involved in winning and your likelihood of victory. Talking to someone who has held office or run for office many times should give you a good sense of the difficulties, but you should also be attentive to the particular characteristics of the office for which you may run and the opponent(s) you may face.

Conclusion: Five Things to Know before You Start

1. Local involvement should not start with the campaign.

Before you start, get involved with local politics and local organizations to learn more about and establish yourself in your community.

2. Learn about the people of your community and their concerns.

Before the campaign, find out more about the characteristics of the community, local problems, and proposed solutions. Make sure the perspectives you hear reflect the differences of opinion and the controversies in your community.

3. Start to build a base of support.

Identify individuals and groups who are likely to support your candidacy. Tell them you are thinking of running and involve them in your decision-making process.

■ BRIGHT IDEA: Approach Potential Supporters Early

Ideally, potential coalition members should be approached before you announce your candidacy or shortly thereafter. This can give you a sense of your support base before you commit to a full campaign. Early coalition-building efforts make groups feel involved in your decision-making process and more committed to the campaign. Research the interests and concerns of groups in your community; remember, the outreach process is about identifying and responding to people's concerns.

4. Know the difficulties before you enter the race.

Be aware of the difficult tasks that all candidates face and how your specific weaknesses might affect your candidacy.

5.   Take your decision to be a candidate seriously.

Instead of deciding to run for office on a whim, be realistic about the challenges and rewards of running and involve others when making your decision.

Planning Your Campaign

2

17

A political campaign is a significant undertaking that involves many people, events, and decisions. Waging a successful campaign requires organized leadership and careful planning. You will have to make a lot of decisions well in advance and prepare to respond to potential problems that may or may not arise.

For this reason, think through the important steps in the process, determine how you will allocate your key resources (time and money), delegate responsibilities for different aspects of the campaign, and have options ready when things do not turn out as planned. Your campaign plan should incorporate each of these elements.

Getting on the Ballot

Take care to establish yourself as an official candidate before publicly launching your campaign. Even though the process is simple, waiting until the last minute to file your candidacy papers is a recipe for disaster. To ensure the viability of your candidacy, always pay close attention to the legal requirements associated with running for office.

Know and Comply with Basic Filing Deadlines and Requirements

You will need to comply with two separate sets of legal deadlines: one for filing candidacy papers, and one for filing campaign contribution and expenditure reports (both are discussed in Chapter 8).

Do not rely on someone to do this for you. Know the legal requirements and keep track of them yourself. You can get copies of the election calendar, which has the filing dates relevant to the office for which you are running, from your local elections official or registrar of voters. The California Fair Political Practices Commission's Web site (www.fppc.ca.gov) has a calendar of filing dates for campaign finance reports. Local jurisdictions may have special election dates and special filing dates, so always check with your local elections official. You can find links to information about these deadlines at campaigns.berkeley.edu.

> ■ **TAKE NOTE: Pay very close attention to deadlines.**
>
> Failure to file complete candidacy papers on time can be fatal to your candidacy.

To be an official candidate for office, you will need to formally announce your intention to run for office by filing a Declaration of Candidacy and Nominating Petitions with your local elections official. Before you begin soliciting money for your campaign, you will need to file a Candidate Intention Statement (FPPC Form 501), which announces to the FPPC the name of the office you are raising money for. (See Chapter 8 for a detailed discussion of these and other legal requirements associated with running for office.)

> ■ **TAKE NOTE: There are also restrictions on who can sign and who can collect signatures for you.**
>
> Not everyone qualifies as a collector! And not just anyone can sign your candidacy papers!

Your Declaration of Candidacy and Nominating Petitions must be filed on time or your candidacy will be ended before it begins. The nominating petitions require signatures of support from registered voters in the jurisdiction where you are running.

Many potential candidates have been shocked when their candidacy papers were rejected as invalid because some of the signatures were from nonresidents or they did not meet other technical requirements. If that happens and it is too late for you to revise your papers in time to meet the filing deadline, you will be precluded from running for office.

If you file your Candidate Intention Statement (FPPC Form 501) late, you will be subject to a stiff fine, and you may have to return illegally raised campaign contributions, but you will be allowed to continue your candidacy.

Developing a Campaign Plan

The best way to make sure your campaign runs smoothly is to do as much planning in advance as possible. Successful candidates typically write a full campaign plan before they begin and regularly refer to it to measure success and make adjustments as the campaign progresses. Planning entails more than simply writing down a list of goals. Decide how to allocate your time, money, and other campaign resources and identify ways to implement your key objectives.

■ ADVICE FROM PROFESSIONALS: "Planning to Win: Strategic Thinking for Local Elections," by Mary Hughes

Football teams have playbooks; symphonies have scores; start-up companies rely on a business plan. So it follows that candidates for public office need a strategic plan that charts a path to victory.

Too often, local candidates fail to write down their research and conclusions in a plan. Writing the rationale for the candidacy, evaluating the constituency's voter history, assessing "the numbers" needed to win all provide a solid basis on which to decide how a campaign will win.

"It's up here," says the manager, pointing to his head. "Too much to do," says the candidate, anxious about fundraising.

Big mistake.

A good strategic plan focuses scarce resources efficiently and eliminates efforts and expenditures that don't yield votes.

As important, it's fun.

Campaigns for local office rarely have the resources to do polling or to hire message mavens or media consultants. But by asking and answering basic questions, local candidates can design and execute a solid strategic campaign plan with the same precision and clarity that marks a winning (and expensive) campaign for Congress.

How will we win? What will we do? The answers to these questions form the core of a strategic plan. The strategic (not including structure or operations) elements of a Campaign Plan for local office are:

- Contest, Context, and Climate
- Candidate, Voters, and Vote Trends
- Competitive Advantages
- Message, Voter Communication, and Field
- Budget, Finance Plan, and Timeline

Contest, Context, and Climate

- ### What kind of contest is it?

The campaign is either about change or maintaining the status quo —do voters want to keep the current mayor or elect a new one?—or it is a contest between different versions of the future, the one your campaign offers voters versus that of your opponent.

An incumbent might argue that voters should let her "finish what we started" and highlight accomplishments and projects in progress. A challenger would argue that we "need a new direction" and offer alternative approaches to old problems.

Candidates for open seats often emphasize their ideological and policy differences, asking voters to embrace their vision.

- ### What is the electoral context for the race?

Is it a presidential or gubernatorial election year? Voter turnout, and therefore the campaign's vote goal, is higher in a presidential election year. Is this a partisan candidacy attached to other popular/unpopular members of the party? Or is it a nonpartisan candidacy that allows for endorsements and alliances on both sides?

- ### A word about electoral climate.

Rarely are individual, local contests determined by the general sentiment of the electorate, but it does happen. The Gingrich revolution of 1994 and the 2003 California recall election are two recent examples. Is there a wave of voter emotion that could toss the campaign boat or create an opportunity?

Candidate, Voters, and Vote Trends

- ### What's the rationale for this candidacy?

Voters deserve a clear and concise answer. Campaign planners should research the candidate's contribution to the community. To understand what motivates the candidate, have her write a faux obituary.

To craft an honest and persuasive answer to "Why are you running?" the candidate must be able to say, clearly and directly: What she is for.

What she has done, and what she will do. Why voters should believe her. Who will stand with her. When the candidate can respond effectively to each of these, the campaign can begin to craft its message.

- ## How many votes do you need to win?

   Past election results hold the key to future campaign success. List vendors can help pinpoint how many and who voted in past similar elections (presidential, gubernatorial, or special?). Project the turnout and calculate the 50% + 1 vote in a two person race or the plurality needed in a multi-candidate race. That's the vote goal.

- ## Where will these votes come from?

   Where do these likely voters reside? From this data the campaign can generate precinct lists for calling and canvassing voters. What common characteristics suggest target groups of votes? Parents? Women? Seniors? New voters? Occasional voters?

   It's important to assess who and what these voters supported in past elections. What else is on the ballot? Will these individuals or issues bring new voters to the polls? Decrease turnout? Split the community? Does your opinion of these candidates or ballot issues matter to voters?

Competitive Advantages

Voters choose candidates for a variety of reasons, not solely because they agree on issues. Examples of other voter considerations are:

- **Age: How does the candidate's age compare to the electorate? Could voters conclude she is too old or young to perform in office?**
- **Gender: Is this a "year of the woman"? Or newcomer? Or incumbent?**
- **Ideology: Does this candidate share the voter's basic philosophy?**
- **Geography: Is this candidate from "my side of town"?**

Other voter criteria to consider: candidate experience, style, race/ethnicity, public and private accomplishments, alliances.

What are the candidate's advantages or disadvantages? Identifying the criteria through which the candidate most clearly connects with voters provides context, direction and tone for communication.

Message, Voter Communication, and Field

- ### What is the point on which the campaign and voters most agree?
Consider the climate of the election, the candidate's rationale for her candidacy, voters' past election choices, the most advantageous criteria of choice. Factor in hot community issues and the focus of the job sought. From these, a campaign's message should emerge.

And whether the underlying message is "We can do better" or "Accountability now," the most effective communication of the message is brief and comparative. Cast the candidate in the most positive light while suggesting a shortcoming in the opponent: "Every school board needs a parent."

- ### Deliver the message by methods that have a track record of success with your voters—mail, phone calls, and volunteer visits are tried and true.
Newspaper ads, billboards and lawn signs work in some areas and are viewed as visual pollution in others.

Layer and reinforce. Low-cost communication like e-newsletters, newspaper inserts, and columns for club newspapers are popular supplements to paid communication.

- ### The plan should include specific responsibility for recruiting, training, managing, and appreciating volunteers.
How and when to deploy them becomes the field plan. Assessing whether canvassing, phone calls, personal "dear neighbor" postcards, or lawn sign delivery is the best use of volunteer time should depend, in part, on the message (if it's personal service and accessibility, a volunteer at the door becomes the message) and practicality. Older volunteers will likely come back for more mailing parties and phone calls, but not precinct walking.

Budget, Finance Plan, and Timeline

- When the campaign has decided on the message and how to communicate it, the next task is figuring out how much it will cost and where those funds will come from.

More than anything else, the budget is a statement of strategy. It should include projected expenditures for staff, headquarters rent and overhead, legal advice, and voter communication materials. Ideally, 70 percent of the budget will be spent on communication with 10 percent set aside for unexpected expenses.

- The finance plan should assign amounts that the campaign can raise through direct mail, events, major donor solicitations, peer solicitation, political action committee contributions, and on-line campaigns.

The budget number and finance plan objective should match. Weekly goals and check-ins are essential to stay on track.

- Finally, all the "to dos" that resulted from researching, analyzing, and formulating the best ways to persuade voters should be laid out on a timeline: everything from when to announce high visibility endorsements to when to order the voter walk lists.

The timeline should include filing deadlines, financial report due dates, and critical events such as debates. When all the important deadlines are visible, the strategy should be clear. Then, there's just the doing and the winning.

Mary Hughes, president of Staton & Hughes, is a veteran Democratic political strategist and campaign advisor based in San Francisco.

A Timeline for Your Campaign

- ### Early

In the early weeks of your campaign, you will need to make progress on several fronts.

- Create an effective core organization to run your campaign (see Chapter 3).
- Establish the substance of your communications by developing your campaign theme and positions on priority issues (see Chapter 4).
- Begin to implement your fundraising plan and to identify contributors (see Chapter 5).
- Develop ways to deliver your message; schedule important events and appearances for the remainder of your campaign (see Chapter 6).
- Build support for your candidacy; talk to important local organizations and leaders and try to gain their endorsements.
- Increase your name recognition by placing large signs at high-traffic intersections and distributing other campaign paraphernalia to supporters.
- Locate your target audiences, develop responses to their concerns, and start talking directly to voters (see Chapter 7).

- ### Middle

Once these efforts are underway, your campaign's focus should turn to getting your message out to key constituencies and persuading undecided voters to vote for you.

- Identify likely supporters and undecided voters and determine how many voters are committed to you and to your opponent(s).
- Actively contact undecided voters through phone, door-to-door, and mail communications and persuade them to vote for you.
- Build your fundraising networks and volunteer base to ensure that there are sufficient resources for your final push.
- Participate in public forums and debates. If none are scheduled, encourage local organizations, members of the news media, and your fellow candidate(s) to organize and participate in future forums.

- **End**

During the final weeks of the campaign, your activities should focus on encouraging likely supporters to vote (by promoting absentee voting and organizing get-out-the-vote efforts on Election Day) and persuading undecided voters that you are the right candidate.

- Target your persuasive efforts to achieve the necessary margin of victory.
- Put your advertising and direct voter contact operations into high gear.
- Create momentum for your campaign by earning free appearances on local media and holding large events that draw many voters.
- Hone your message as voters pay more attention to the campaign.

Producing a Campaign Budget

Successful candidates create budgets to ensure the efficient allocation of their campaign resources. Without a plan you might spend too much money on overhead or administration and too little on communicating your message to voters, or you might overspend in the beginning of the campaign and not retain enough resources to make a strong finish. The key to successful budgeting is making a realistic assessment of your fundraising targets and the costs of implementing your campaign plan.

Start by projecting the amount of money you expect to raise over the course of the campaign, including when contributions are likely to come in. You should make an informed guess, an optimistic assessment, a conservative assessment, and a worst-case scenario and establish basic budget allocations using each estimate. The actual fundraising for most campaigns falls somewhere between the informed guess and the conservative estimate. Budget carefully, so that you don't end up incurring large debts by the end of the campaign or lose your final opportunity to speak to voters.

Next, make a list of all the items that are absolutely necessary to your campaign. This might include office space, salaries, materials, travel, mail, and fundraising. Typical fundraising estimates suggest that nearly one-third of the money you raise will be spent on your efforts to raise it. No matter how you might want to spend the money that you raise, these up-front costs must be in your budget.

Finally, divide your remaining funds between delivering your message and building your organization. You should allocate as much money as possible to communicating your message to the voters. Your biggest expenditure will probably be electronic media advertising, though many local campaigns often operate without this. Television and radio advertisements entail costs associated with production, ad placement, and professional expertise, which can be quite expensive.

Depending on the size and location of your constituency, print advertising, direct mail, phone contact, and door-to-door canvassing may be more cost-effective methods of contacting voters than electronic media. (See Chapter 6 for more on the costs associated with delivering your message.)

You can use volunteers to get your message out, but remember they are not without cost. Typically, volunteers must be called regularly by a staff member, given materials to distribute, and provided with refreshments to thank them for their time and effort and encourage them to offer their help again.

> ■ **LEARN MORE ON THE WEB:**
>
> At **campaigns.berkeley.edu** you will find more information on campaign plans and budgets, including examples.

However you decide to allocate your funds, careful budgeting is critical to your campaign's success. When developing your budget, be aware of all your potential expenditures, be realistic when assessing their likely costs, and keep track of your spending very carefully. If your estimates turn out to be off, revise your budget allocations to account for the difference.

Allocating Your Time

When you are a candidate, your time is your most valuable resource. You are typically the best fundraiser, the best persuader, and the best organizer. The campaign revolves around you, and people look to you for leadership. At the start of the campaign, you may have time to be involved in all aspects of the campaign, but as the election draws near your time will grow increasingly scarce and ever more precious. Managing your time effectively will enable you to focus on and complete the most important tasks of your campaign.

To ensure your time is allocated effectively, keep a precise schedule of your campaign duties and engagements. This will help you keep track of your many obligations. It will also reduce the chance that you will forget to attend an event that you promised to attend, which can result in losing the support of those who invited you and make a bad impression on those who came to see you. Always be on time to meetings with voters, campaign events, and other scheduled engagements. By doing so, you will develop a reputation as someone who cares about the concerns of the voters.

As you make decisions about your schedule, you will not be able to accept every invitation. You will be asked to attend multiple events at the same time, especially the closer you are to the election. More important engagements may arise from time to time, forcing you to cancel previously scheduled appearances. If you do have to cancel, make sure you contact those who invited you as early as possible, provide a clear explanation of the reason for your cancellation, and propose alternate times to make up for your absence. Hiring a staff person or designating a volunteer to serve as your scheduler makes this process much easier.

> ■ **TAKE NOTE:**
>
> Time is your most precious campaign asset. Track your time carefully. And use it wisely.

Some things to keep in mind when planning your schedule:

- Allocate sufficient time for making fundraising calls and attending fundraisers.
- Look through a list of community events, fairs, and parades to make sure you don't miss a major opportunity to meet potential voters.
- Make yourself available for any public forums, especially if other candidates will be there. The public is wary of candidates who seem to avoid debates and other opportunities for public dialogue.
- Make yourself widely available to the media at their convenience. Any opportunity to appear on radio or television, even for a short time, can save your campaign money (for example, the cost of buying TV time) and introduce you to many voters at once.
- Include in your schedule time to rest and enjoy family life. Take time to replenish your body and spirit. It will make you a more effective campaigner.

Planning the Kick-Off Event

A campaign is composed of a series of events designed to communicate your message to voters and interest them in your candidacy. Campaign events can be an effective way to get media attention, rally your supporters, and create "news" by making important public statements. Your first opportunity to achieve these goals is your campaign kick-off event. The local media often consider the announcement of a political candidacy to be an event worthy of coverage, and supporters will get excited when you make your intentions clear and launch your campaign.

The kick-off event may also provide the media and your supporters with their first impression of you as a candidate. Take advantage of the free publicity and make sure the initial impression is favorable. Hold the event near the beginning of the week at a location that is public, provides "good pictures" (dramatic backdrops or large crowds help to ensure coverage), and is easy to find. Inform your supporters and the press about your event several days in advance.

The goal of the kick-off event is to create a "buzz" about your candidacy so it becomes a topic of discussion among your supporters and local stakeholders. You might invite a popular public official or someone who is well known and respected in the community to introduce you, which can add credibility to your candidacy. In your announcement speech, make sure that you provide a clear rationale for your candidacy. (See Chapter 4 for more on developing your campaign rationale.) You should also provide evidence of your knowledge of community issues and concerns and describe how you plan to address them. Set aside time to meet with press after the event, in order to answer specific questions about your candidacy.

Your kick-off event does not have to be limited to a single press conference. Instead, you might create a day of events to keep the momentum flowing in your favor. For example, you might hold events in several neighborhoods or in conjunction with some early precinct walking. Ideally, your kick off event will be the first of a series of campaign events held throughout the campaign.

■ ADVICE FROM THE FRONT LINES: "How to Lose and Win an Election," by Polly Armstrong

I was a shoe-in when I ran for my second term on the city council in
1996. I had lived in my district for 20 years. I'd spent the eight years pre-
ceding my first term as the council aide for the district. I'd run May Fairs
and Campfire groups, League of Women Voters meetings, and PTA meetings. I had received newspaper endorsements and good publicity on my
accomplishments in my first two-year term. I was an incumbent and the
gentleman running against me was unknown. All conventional wisdom
said I would not need to run an active campaign, and I didn't.

On election night I lost the race by about 25 votes to the now quite
well known opponent. Fortunately for me, postelection day counting of
absentee ballots pushed me ahead by 90 votes and my political life re-
sumed, but I was humbled and confused by my narrow victory and set
out to analyze what had gone wrong.

The answer was depressingly simple, really. Although my opponent
had little money and no quality literature, he had been tenacious. He and
a dedicated supporter had knocked on doors in my traditionally strong
precincts, dropped amateur literature on doorsteps across the district, and
talked to voters every day and most evenings throughout the campaign.
They managed to contact most residents at least twice and sometimes
more often. Even people who knew me and approved of my work were
impressed by their dedication and earnestness.

In addition to having a stronger ground game, my opponent also ap-
pealed to specific segments of my district. About half of my district's
voters are tenants or students who live on the University of California
campus. My opponent's pro rent control position held an automatic appeal to tenants, and the fact that my opponent was a Green Party member
surely trumped my Democratic registration among some voters. I wasn't
willing to change my stance on rent control or my party identification for
the next campaign, but I certainly could and had to do a better job of contacting voters the next time I ran.

After I decided to run for a third term, I developed a new game plan
that incorporated the lessons of my narrow victory. My physical condi-
tion did not permit me to trudge up and down the many steep hills and

stairs in my district, so I began my voter outreach by having neighborhood meetings at voters' homes a year and half before the election. One week before the meetings, volunteers dropped flyers at every house within a 10-block radius announcing the meeting. Afterward we dropped flyers again, reporting on what we talked about at the meeting. Attendance was very light—perhaps an average of eight people per meeting—but by the time we were done, I had contacted hundreds of voters twice.

Over the course of my term, I developed other ways to keep my name before the voters. I designed brightly colored single sheet statements on my positions on local issues and passed them out at every opportunity. I produced and delivered newsletters four times a year to keep voters informed about what was happening at City Hall. I paid for these newsletters with campaign funds, not city money, and they were very popular.

Most of the fraternities and sororities on campus are in my district, and I made a lot of house visits for dinners and talks and tried to find other ways to connect with them. Eventually I hired a Greek coordinator to get out the vote and developed literature specific to campus issues. (Depressingly, after the election I learned that none of my campus efforts had increased student turnout among the Greek community or students in general.)

Eighteen months before the election, I formed a committee with four strong supporters and a campaign chair. We met monthly for the first six months and then weekly to discuss strategy and plan campaign events. Over the course of the campaign I raised approximately $30,000 (in a district with 11,000 residents) through mailed fundraising letters and two campaign parties—one expensive and fancy, one local and simple—so that anyone who wanted to support me financially would have a comfortable way to do it. This gave me the resources I needed to get my message out.

In late summer we put out a glossy four-sided flyer that introduced me and my family and my experience to the voters, even though it irritated me to think that all my years in the community hadn't taken care of that! We followed that piece with five or six mailers spread out through the last two months of the campaign, stressing my accomplishments and experience and my opponent's lack thereof. Although the pieces were critical of my opponent, the contrasts that we drew were fair and necessary for underscoring the relevant differences between us.

In the final weeks of the campaign we intensified our efforts to contact voters. I knocked on doors in the neighborhoods where I had not done as well as I should have in '96. If voters weren't home I left a signed card saying, "Sorry I missed you." We also blanketed the district with yard signs. Professionals say they don't matter but they do add energy to a campaign. Our signs were stolen at a prodigious rate but replacing them kept us in personal contact with our supporters.

We knew the person helping my opponent's campaign had a reputation for sending out "hit pieces," so we saved enough money and prepared ourselves to combat a last-minute lie or attack. Not surprisingly, my opponent released an attack piece three days before the election. It included a photo of me with a laser gun from the opening celebration of a laser tag gallery and text indicating I was a dangerous choice for office! We agreed that the piece would be seen as silly rather than convincing, so we spent the money we had saved to respond to his anticipated attack on card-sized reproductions of newspaper endorsement highlights, instead. We covered the student areas with them in the last 24 hours.

On election night I won by a 16% margin (58% to 42%). All my contact work in the neighborhoods that traditionally supported me was successful. Voter turnout increased and the percentage of support that I received was dramatically higher in those areas. There was very little positive change among the tenant and student districts, but my base voters came through for me.

The lessons I learned from this campaign were: campaign even when you don't think you need to, the more voter contact the better, concentrate on the voters who agree with you, and although you need to be prepared to correct an attack, don't start the fight as there are better ways to use your campaign's resources!

Polly Armstrong recently returned to a more peaceful private life after 16 years in Berkeley politics.

Developing Strategy with Campaign Managers and Consultants

Friends and professional advisors can provide valuable help and expertise when building your campaign plan and designing your strategy.

Ultimately, however, it is your name on the ballot and campaign materials. All campaign activities will reflect on you and your candidacy.

As you solicit advice, keep several things in mind: First, you know more than anyone about your personal strengths and weaknesses and how they might affect your run for office. Second, you may know more about the specific concerns of the people in your district or in the jurisdiction where you are running than your advisors, especially if they come from another area. What works in some places may not work in your community. Importing successful strategies from elsewhere can be an effective part of your campaign, but be sure to adapt them to the particular circumstances of your area and your campaign. Third, you may be more concerned about your long-term reputation than an advisor. You should be the final judge of whether or not a possible short-term tactical advantage is worth the risk of long-term damage to your reputation.

Having a candid conversation with your managers and consultants at the beginning of the campaign about what you will and will not do to get elected will help to minimize the likelihood for mid- or late-campaign disagreements. If you think that your consultant is recommending something unethical, check the Code of Ethics promulgated by the American Association of Political Consultants available at our Web site (campaigns.berkeley.edu). The principles articulated in the code may also be a starting point for discussions about campaign philosophy.

> ■ **BEST PRACTICE:**
>
> Sit down early on with your supporters and strategists to establish ethical lines that you will not cross.

Conclusion: Five Things to Know When Planning Your Campaign

1. Context matters.

Every campaign is different and must respond to the specific context in which it is run. Be sensitive to the concerns, values, and political culture of your constituency and know how to adapt the key strategic elements of a campaign to your race.

2. Take care of important details.

Getting on the ballot and filling out campaign finance forms may not seem like the most central aspects of your campaign, but failure to comply with the legal requirements associated with running for office can sink your candidacy.

3. Plan as much as possible in advance of the campaign.

As the campaign progresses, you may not have time to engage in lengthy brainstorming sessions to determine the scope and direction of your campaign. Before the campaign begins, develop your basic strategy and how you will implement your objectives. Make sure your plan is coherent, allows for mid-course corrections as conditions change, and achieves your key goals.

4. Manage your time and money carefully.

Your time and the funds you raise for your campaign are key assets of your candidacy. They must be managed like the major resources they are. Develop and follow a realistic campaign budget and carefully schedule your time throughout the campaign.

5. Set goals and monitor progress.

Based on your campaign plan, make clear what you, your staff, and your volunteers are expected to accomplish in terms of voter outreach, fundraising targets, or office responsibilities. Monitor your progress, celebrate your successes, and adjust your plans to the shifting context of your campaign.

Building Your Campaign Organization

3

Successful campaigns, like most major projects, require well-run organizations that make the most of participants' talents and skills and combine them in a way that promotes collective success. As a candidate, your achievements will be the product of a team effort.

In order for you to focus on communicating your message to voters, you will need to build an organization that will manage the bulk of the operational and administrative tasks of the campaign for you. While a team of volunteers can provide much needed support to your campaign, running a successful political campaign requires expertise. If possible, build an organization that combines professionals and volunteers—trusted specialists who direct your campaign and a motivated group of beginners who build a broad movement of local support for your candidacy.

Selecting Staff for Key Campaign Positions

Start building your organization by filling your key positions and then add help where it is most needed. Here are the most important roles to fill in your campaign, in order of importance:

- ### Campaign Manager

The campaign manager is responsible for all aspects of the campaign. Initially, the campaign manager will be intimately involved in developing campaign strategy and planning your campaign. After the planning phase, the campaign manager's role will shift from strategy development to strategy implementation, making adjustments as necessary to achieve the ultimate goal of winning the election.

Qualifications include an understanding of political strategy, a mutual trust and rapport with the candidate, good organizational abilities (including management and delegation skills), objectivity about the candidate and the campaign (which may make loved ones inappropriate campaign managers), and the ability to deliver unwelcome information. The campaign manager needs to share the candidate's vision of what are —and are not—acceptable campaign practices.

• Treasurer

In most races, your treasurer is legally responsible for keeping track of your contributions and expenditures. Your treasurer should be a person you trust and should have experience in handling money. If you have a friend who is an accountant, he or she should be the first person you ask.

Since campaign financing procedures are somewhat different from those used in the business world, someone with previous campaign finance experience will provide a significant advantage. Whoever you choose, make sure that he or she is willing to commit for the length of the campaign so that you won't need to transfer responsibility for bookkeeping while the campaign is underway.

> ■ **TAKE NOTE:**
>
> The campaign manager and the candidate need to share a vision of what are – and are not – acceptable campaign practices.

The first thing your campaign treasurer should do is read all the regulations that apply to the office for which you are a candidate. These are usually available from the county elections official; links to relevant Web sites can be found at campaigns.berkeley.edu. Make sure that you and your treasurer are aware of the full scope and timing of your filing responsibilities and check-in with your treasurer regularly to ensure that your campaign finance reports have been filed on time.

• Fundraising Director

In small campaigns, the treasurer may also assume the role of fundraising director. Appointing a separate fundraising director, however, can increase your total level of contributions. The fundraising director is responsible for implementing the fundraising plan. This involves coordinating all of the tools at the campaign's disposal to meet fundraising goals within the necessary time frame. The fundraising director guides the campaign's major donor and direct mail fundraising programs and oversees fundraising events. In campaigns that cannot afford an accountant or attorney, the fundraising director must have a basic knowledge of campaign finance regulations.

• Volunteer Coordinator

This person is responsible for recruiting, scheduling, and organizing the volunteer team. Qualifications include good organizational and scheduling skills, coaching skills (for volunteers with limited or no prior campaign experience), diplomacy, patience, and a commitment to ongoing communications with the campaign's volunteers.

The volunteer coordinator must be a motivator and a source of accountability with the troops. In larger campaigns, candidates may want to split responsibility for managing volunteers between a volunteer coordinator and a field coordinator, with the field coordinator assuming primary responsibility for implementing the voter contact program.

• Scheduler

The scheduler helps manage the candidate's time. He or she responds to outside requests for candidate appearances and searches for speaking opportunities where the candidate might make an impact on prospective voters. The scheduler is the campaign's primary contact with the local media but should not be the person who makes statements on behalf of the candidate.

The scheduler should be organized and personable, preferably with experience as an administrative assistant or in public relations. In small campaigns, this person might also serve as the office manager.

Hiring Other Paid Staff

Most small campaigns will not have enough funds to hire people for all of the positions listed above. Larger campaigns should consider hiring several additional employees whom the candidate can depend upon. This is because volunteers typically work fewer hours and serve at their own convenience, and many tasks, especially on a large campaign, require a full-time commitment.

An office manager can help ease the administrative tasks of the other staff. This person might help organize materials, send out mailings, and answer phone calls. Depending on your campaign strategy, you may want to have an outreach person to oversee your efforts to contact voters using phone banks or door-to-door canvassing. In small campaigns, the volunteer coordinator will take on these roles. You may want a Web master to build and maintain your Web site, especially if you plan to regularly update your site with new statements and respond to email requests and questions. You might assign someone to post signs throughout the district or jurisdiction for at least part of the campaign. This person would deliver yard signs to supporters who request them, and search for prime locations to post larger signs, which will help increase your name identification.

One way to expand your staff without exceeding your payroll allowance is to assign official positions to volunteers. Strong supporters or local party organizers, especially young people, may be willing to take on extra responsibilities if they are given an official internship or title in the campaign. Volunteers of this kind should be treated as staff members and thanked repeatedly.

Setting Up the Office

Your organization needs a center of operations. If possible, rent inexpensive office space that is accessible to your volunteers and visible to the community. Start a separate bank account for the campaign, obtain a campaign credit card, and keep track of office expenditures (for example, rent, furniture, phone service, Internet service account), even if they are donated by an organization as an in-kind contribution.

For a small campaign, the headquarters might be a room in your house. Even if you have limited resources, try to create a space with at least a phone line, a computer, and a printer. The campaign room should have the appearance of a professional operation. It should be a place where volunteers receive clear task assignments and there is an abundance of campaign supplies on hand. At a minimum, make sure that you keep your materials organized.

Maintain databases of contributors, volunteers, and media contacts. Have contribution envelopes, signs, and legal forms on hand. Obtain a precinct map of your district or jurisdiction to locate your target voters and follow your progress in door-to-door campaigning. Compile a stack of favorable media clippings about the campaign that volunteers can xerox and distribute to interested voters.

Create a file of information about yourself and your fellow candidate(s). These files can serve as reference points, helping to ensure the accuracy of the claims you make during the campaign. Post a large calendar on the wall to keep track of events and responsibilities. Most importantly, balance your books daily and make sure that your database allows you to record every debit from and credit to your campaign accounts.

■ **BEST PRACTICE:**

Never ask a volunteer to do something that is illegal, unethical, or you would never do yourself.

Recruiting Volunteers

Building a large volunteer base for your campaign is an effective strategy that costs little, enhances your public image, reduces the strain on you and your paid staff, and gives supporters an important opportunity to participate directly in getting you elected.

Getting started with your recruiting can be difficult because the most important resource for gaining new volunteers is existing volunteers. The good news is that once you get your operations going and treat your volunteers well, your support base is likely to grow. At the beginning of your campaign, however, you may need to rely on your friendship networks and existing organizations for volunteers.

As you work within the local structure of your political party or participate in events for social or charitable organizations prior to running for office, develop a list of potential helpers that you can call on when you begin campaigning. If you have already built a coalition of supporters, ask your coalition partners to recruit volunteers for your campaign. Student organizations at local schools provide another venue for recruiting volunteers, as do local political and social clubs.

■ **BEST PRACTICE: Build a large volunteer base for your campaign.**

Building a broad campaign organization not only helps you win elections by contacting more voters and mobilizing your base of support, it strengthens democracy. By expanding participation, you give your supporters an opportunity to take control of the future of their community by participating directly in local decision making.

Teaming up with other campaigns can offer an effective way to multiply your volunteer resources. Consider contacting candidates who are running for other offices in your district or jurisdiction. See if they would be willing to combine their leaflet-dropping efforts and other forms of contact with voters with those of your campaign. Always circulate a volunteer sign up sheet at campaign events and meetings with voters.

One way to encourage participation is to make the first event of the campaign season entertaining. If your initial fundraiser involves free food and music, for example, it is usually easy to get people to help with the planning. If you make precinct walking a social activity that is friendly to families, you are likely to get people to commit to a regular schedule.

Whenever you recruit new volunteers make sure that you get all of their contact information, including phone numbers and email addresses. Put their names and contact information in a volunteer database along with the types of activities they are interested in doing and their hours of availability. If people cannot attend the event that you are recruiting them for, take down their information and extend regular invitations until they find an event that they can attend. It is best to have at least a few activities that can be done on a weekly basis so that you can get several volunteers to develop a habit of coming in every week and recruiting others to come along.

As people volunteer their time for your campaign, make sure their contributions are recognized. Introduce volunteers to your campaign staff and your supporters and make sure that they get some face time with you, the candidate they are trying to help. As the election draws nearer, emphasize to volunteers who have been with you since the beginning that the current volunteer projects are more critical than those that came earlier, making their help even more valuable. Invite your volunteers to campaign functions that do not involve work, so that they can share in your success as the campaign progresses.

■ **BRIGHT IDEA: Repudiate Unethical Activities**

Make sure that everyone in your campaign adheres to your high ethical standards. Many campaign codes of conduct address this issue by committing the candidate to disavow unethical activities. For example, California's Code of Campaign Conduct, which many candidates sign, states:

I shall immediately and publicly repudiate support deriving from any individual or group which resorts, on behalf of my candidacy or in opposition to that of my opponent, to the methods and tactics which I condemn. I shall accept responsibility to take firm action against any subordinate who violates any provision of this code or the laws governing elections.

Of course, it is better to avoid having to disavow unethical activities by making it clear to your supporters and volunteers up front what kind of campaign you plan to conduct and what kinds of activities are not acceptable. Stress that, while you appreciate their commitment to your shared cause, if anyone steps over the line, you will have to repudiate their actions immediately and publicly.

■ ADVICE FROM THE FRONT LINES: "Why I Volunteered," by Katie Burke

I volunteered to work for Tom when he decided to run as a challenger in the mayor's race because he asked me to, and his request carried considerable weight. I first met Tom while working on another campaign, where he had been a strong motivating force among the volunteers. I respected him, and when he asked me to work for him I felt a personal stake in the election. Tom told me that students' voices, my voice, mattered in this election. He told me that I could help him reach students. I felt empowered, and I believed in him, so I volunteered.

As a student organizer, I began volunteering by door-knocking, phone banking to student communities, and going with Tom to meet student organizations and ask for their support. As my dedication to Tom's campaign grew, so did my responsibility—my part-time involvement quickly became a full-time commitment. I was soon organizing call nights with volunteers from supportive student organizations, and I developed a comprehensive database of student volunteers and supporters. I recruited volunteers on campus, managed student phone bankers, and worked with the campaign staff to develop a call script that would most effectively convey Tom's message to students.

I found it easy to advocate for a candidate I knew, to a constituency I knew, in a community I knew. Voter contact was straightforward and felt personal. The conversations I had with students after knocking on their doors felt very similar to political discussions that we might have had in a political science class. I could tell likely voters exactly why I was going to vote for Tom and why I thought that they should too.

Tom promised if elected mayor he would work to increase the amount of affordable housing available to students who are faced with a tight rental market, and he would work to protect low fares for public transportation. When speaking with my peers, it was easy to show that these were not abstract political issues, but rather "our issues"—practical matters with which most students had direct experience. As a member of their community, I was able to relate to student voters through our shared concerns. Familiarity and first-hand knowledge of the candidate further boosted my confidence while engaged in voter persuasion.

There were times, however, when I became a little nervous while speaking with voters about Tom's stances on particular issues. The pressure to provide specific and accurate information on a multitude of issues (including issues that I, a college student, had no direct experience with) to a questioning voter can be a little overwhelming. While it is probably not possible to know exactly where a candidate stands on every single issue, I was able to speak from my own experience and tell them who Tom was as a person and as a candidate. In addition to listening to me describe his campaign platform, many voters were receptive to becoming acquainted with Tom in this way.

I believe my membership in the community that I was seeking to organize, and the credibility that came from this, as well as my personal connection to the candidate made me a more effective voice for Tom's campaign. I also developed a unique sense of accountability to my peers, which increased my commitment to the campaign. It was as if the campaign promises had become my promises. I knew that the role of a volunteer is to aide the campaign in spreading its message and executing its strategy, not to question it. While engaged in voter persuasion among my own student population, however, it was important for me to know that student issues really were a significant part of the campaign and would be addressed by Tom's administration if he won.

Fortunately, from spending time in the campaign office and listening to Tom and the rest of the staff discuss the campaign, I knew this was the case. Knowing that the goals of the candidate were also top priorities for my community motivated me to work even harder as a volunteer, for both the candidate and my community.

Katie Burke is a graduate of the University of California at Berkeley and currently works as a congressional aide on Capitol Hill.

Using Volunteers Effectively

Volunteers provide valuable, free labor to your campaign. Make every effort to use this resource wisely by planning effective and creative ways to incorporate volunteers into the major tasks of the campaign. Make these tasks fun (for example, play music, provide refreshments), so volunteers are likely to return.

Volunteers are always needed for mailing fundraising letters, making phone calls, walking precincts, delivering signs, and writing thank you notes. At the very least, your volunteer coordinator should organize these types of activities for your volunteers and be prepared to have enough work on hand for as much help as you might receive. Keep in mind that for some projects, especially ones that are critical to the success of the campaign, you may need to hire a professional.

Volunteers can be used in innovative ways. They can seek out local organizations to talk to about your candidacy, pass out campaign materials at busy locations, produce additional materials for your Web site, prepare briefings on local policy issues, return phone calls and emails from voters, set up a booth or table at a local event to publicize your candidacy, and prepare specialized versions of your campaign material for specific events or constituencies. Always explain the necessity and importance of the activity that you are asking volunteers to complete, and match the skills of the volunteer to the task at hand.

Volunteers will—wholly apart from these tasks—influence a circle of friends and family to vote for you, just by their commitment to your candidacy. They should be fully informed so that they feel a part of the campaign organization and can promote your candidacy in their discussions.

Volunteers are an important source of feedback about how well a candidate's messages and strategies are working in the field. After a day of precinct walking or phone banking, ask your volunteers to report on how voters responded to their efforts. Request their suggestions for how to improve future efforts and give them credit for their good ideas.

■ ADVICE FROM PROFESSIONALS: "Building an Effective Volunteer Program," by Jarryd Gonzales

All campaigns have volunteers. Winning campaigns understand the impact an effective volunteer program can have on the outcome of a race. Volunteers play a significant role on local campaigns, more so than statewide or national campaigns, because local campaigns often operate on very limited budgets. There are many components to every campaign plan, most of which are paid efforts such as: radio or television ads, direct mail and telemarketing. Perhaps not as sexy, but equally important to all campaigns, is the volunteer program.

There are four steps to building an effective volunteer program:

1. Recruiting
2. Managing
3. Tasking
4. Thanking

1. Recruiting

Volunteers are the heart and soul of any campaign team. Unlike paid staff, volunteers receive no monetary compensation and dedicate their free time to a cause they believe is right—getting you elected!

There is a misperception that lack of time and cynicism have resulted in a decline of volunteerism on political campaigns. The number one reason people do not volunteer is because we don't ask!

Recruiting volunteers willing to dedicate their spare time to your cause is not as daunting as it seems. In order to effectively recruit volunteers, it is important to understand why people volunteer.

Reasons People Volunteer:

*   Commitment to particular political party/ideology
*   Commitment to a specific candidate
*   Commitment to a specific issue
*   People dislike your opponent
*   Community service requirement

Now that you have an idea of why people volunteer, the following are good resources for volunteer recruitment:

Family and Friends

Always begin with your personal rolodex or phone list. No one knows the candidate better than his or her family and friends, and they should be the first source of local campaign volunteers. These individuals are typically easy to recruit, loyal to the candidate, and willing to work hard.

College /High School Students

One of the best and often overlooked sources for campaign volunteers is your local college or high school. Political Science majors are
usually eager to get real political experience—students with other majors,
such as journalism, history, and information technology, are also quality
potential volunteers. Political science departments, student governments,
and political clubs can serve as easy points of contact. Some high schools
require that students complete a specific number of community service
hours to graduate. Contacting the American government or civics teacher
at the nearby high school may be worthwhile.

Association Members

Is the candidate an active member of any civic, community, church,
or other group? Members of those groups may be willing to spend their
free time working on the campaign. Members of such organizations are
often knowledgeable about local issues and have large networks of civic-
minded acquaintances.

Local Political Parties

Whether you are a Republican, Democrat, or Green Party member,
your local political party may be able to provide you with names of people who have volunteered in the past, or who have asked to volunteer for
this election. Check with party leaders to see if such lists are available.

Unsolicited Offers

Few people will call a campaign or stop a candidate on the street and
ask to donate money. But many campaigns are surprised by how many
people offer to volunteer their time and talents to the campaign without
being asked. Be prepared for unsolicited offers to volunteer: always carry
small, preprinted cards for potential volunteers to fill out, and make sure
to follow up and involve them in the campaign. Another avenue is the Internet. Be sure to have a volunteer sign-up page on your Web site. You'd
be surprised how many people will sign up to volunteer online.

Volunteer Networks

Make use of the friends and families of your existing volunteer
corps. Ask your volunteers to recruit their friends and family to help with

the race, and provide a creative opportunity for them to do so: Have a Volunteer Appreciation Party for your existing volunteers and ask them to bring friends and family. Be sure to send around a sign-up sheet with specific volunteer tasks on specific dates.

Campaign Events

After asking for votes and/or donations at campaign events, the campaign should ask anyone interested in volunteering to fill out an information card. This recruitment can be done at all kinds of events: the kick-off rally, fundraisers, coffees, town hall debates. If such a solicitation threatens to detract from the main purpose of the event, the recruitment can take place on the way out, by placing tables or staff at the back of the event.

Make your headquarters volunteer-friendly. Have snacks and beverages available at all times, take a photo of every volunteer and post them on a wall entitled "Volunteer Corner," and have a television set or radio for their entertainment while they are working.

2. Managing

Volunteers must be managed. Despite their hard work and dedication, they are not experts and must be overseen. Every campaign that uses volunteers should hire or designate a Volunteer Coordinator whose job is to recruit, manage, schedule and train volunteers. The ideal Volunteer Coordinator works well with people, is a proven motivator, and possesses great patience.

In addition to appointing a Volunteer Coordinator, the campaign should produce a volunteer policy manual that details appropriate attire, acceptable/nonacceptable behavior, working hours, re-imbursement for mileage and other minor expenses (if applicable), and office procedures such as how to answer the telephone or work the fax machine.

3. Tasking

There is nothing worse for a volunteer than arriving at a headquarters where there is nothing to do. This is the fastest way to lose your volunteer base. Be sure to keep a list of tasks for volunteers at all times. Equally important is determining the types of tasks your volunteers ought to be working on.

The following is a list of common volunteer tasks:

- Stuffing mail
- Answering phones
- Phone banking
- Precinct walks/canvassing
- Yard sign delivery
- Data input
- Making copies

Once you have developed a list of volunteer activities, be sure to match them with the skills of your volunteers. An organized campaign will have all volunteers fill-out an information card that asks them to list their areas of interest —for example, computer work, making phone calls, walking precincts, etc.

4. Thanking

The most effective way to retain your volunteers is to thank them. A campaign can recruit hundreds of volunteers, but if they are not thanked, many of your volunteers will not return.

There are many ways to thank volunteers. The candidate can make personal thank you calls to volunteers, or the campaign can host a Volunteer Appreciation Barbeque after a weekend campaign activity. A more expensive avenue might be to take out a one-page ad in your local newspaper and thank your volunteers by listing their names.

Volunteers are the grassroots backbone to every campaign. In addition to augmenting the paid components of a strategic plan, the amount of volunteer activity on a local race says a lot about a campaign and its candidate. Volunteer activity usually means that people are passionate about a candidate and his issues. Often that passion and drive lead to a motivated workforce that will yield positive results on Election Day.

Jarryd Gonzales was political director of the California Republican Party and executive director of Victory 2004.

Building Coalitions with Local Organizations

The easiest way to increase the size of your organization is to enlist the help of other organizations. Rather than recruiting one volunteer at a time, you can encourage entire social clubs, unions, or church groups to help with your campaign. These groups typically have leaders that you can speak to in order to gain their support; the leadership can sometimes do further recruiting on your behalf. Here are a few suggestions for building coalitions with allied organizations:

> ■ **BRIGHT IDEA: Thank Your Volunteers**
>
> Always remember to thank your volunteers during the campaign and after it is over. Before Election Day, think about how you will thank members of your campaign (starting with your victory speech). Providing a personal thank you (email, notes, and phone calls) to those who gave their time and effort to your campaign is not only the right thing to do — it is an investment that will pay off in future campaigns.

- **Connect with potential coalition members early in the campaign.**

  Find out who is involved with and leads groups that might be supportive of your efforts. See if you can meet with the group's leaders and eventually with the entire leadership hierarchy. Be frank about your stand on issues pertaining to the individual organization —this meeting is about building trust and there is nothing to be gained by less than full disclosure. At the same time, identify common ground and areas of agreement. Ask for the public support of the group or an endorsement, if possible. Although some groups may not (or may be legally unable to) support political candidates outright, their leaders may be able to endorse you.

- **Consider creating an advisory board or executive committee.**

  Offer groups a way to participate in campaign planning and discussions by creating an advisory board of group leaders. Use the committee to communicate with the groups that support you, encourage communication between groups, and help group leaders develop an appreciation of the need to form a consensus among disparate elements in the community. Members should be respected and influential representatives of supportive groups and participate in meetings consistently.

- Recognize participants' contributions.

Appreciation goes a long way to motivate busy individuals to help. People like to feel important and know that their efforts make a difference. Different individuals and organizations offer different resources and strengths. All contributions are important. Be sure to acknowledge both the organizations and the individual leaders who assist you.

Conclusion: Five Things to Know When Building Your Organization

1. The candidate cannot do it all.

Running for office is an arduous task. The process will be more manageable—and more successful—if there is a division of labor. In particular, it is helpful to have a campaign manager—someone whose job it is to make sure that the campaign plan is being implemented while keeping an eye on the ultimate objective, which is to win the election. Other useful people to have on your team include a treasurer, a fundraising director, a volunteer coordinator, and a scheduler.

> ■ **BEST PRACTICE: Follow coordination restrictions.**
>
> Remember that if organizations are planning to engage in advertising on your behalf, these efforts must be independent of your campaign, or they will be considered an in-kind contribution to your campaign. If organizations want to help in other ways, such as donating resources and directing volunteers to your campaign, encourage them to participate through your official campaign channels, while following all campaign finance restrictions.

2. Campaigns are about people.

Campaigns are about the candidate and the voters, of course, but volunteers are an important aspect of the campaign. Volunteers perform some of the most critical tasks in a campaign, including voter contact, fundraising, and getting out the vote. Make recruiting volunteers and involving them in your efforts a key goal.

3. Know whom to include.

Friends, family, coworkers and their friends are sources of volunteers, as are organizations that share your vision for the community. Know in advance (as part of your campaign planning process) the types of activities for which you need volunteers. This helps you match volunteers' skills and time availability with tasks, and it ensures that you make prudent and effective use of a most precious resource—people's time.

4. Know whom not to include.

Not everyone who volunteers will be beneficial to the campaign. Avoid people who will discredit the campaign or be a burden. People who are known to be indiscreet are another kind of volunteer to avoid; your volunteers will be privy to sensitive strategic information about the campaign. You need to trust your team to keep this information confidential.

5. Take responsibility without micromanaging.

You are the leader of your campaign. When mistakes are made or the organization is not working effectively, you are responsible for finding ways to make it work better. But trying to manage every detail of the campaign is not a wise use of your time. Give your staff the freedom and flexibility they need to do their jobs.

4

53

Successful candidates win the support of voters by effectively communicating their ideas, aspirations, and qualifications for office to the electorate. They communicate by developing a campaign message that establishes an emotional connection with the voters, so that the voters feel they know the candidate and share his or her beliefs.

Some voters will want to learn all about your issue platform and you should certainly respond to these requests. The vast majority of voters, however, lead busy lives that do not leave much room for becoming well informed about your candidacy or politics in general. Many voters will enter the voting booth knowing only a few pieces of information about you. Ideally, your name on the ballot will remind them of your experience and what you hope to accomplish in office. Making that happen starts with developing a succinct message that gives voters compelling reasons to support you.

Three Elements of an Effective Message

Campaigns are about persuading likely voters to vote for you. To do this, candidates need a compelling message and a strategy for communicating it. (See Chapter 6 for more on how to effectively deliver your message.) A message is not merely a slogan; it is a comprehensive summary of your candidacy. Political consultants advise candidates that there are three elements of a campaign message: (1) the campaign rationale, (2) the campaign theme, and (3) positions on key issues.

Developing Your Rationale

Your campaign rationale is the reason you are running for office. It should be a short (one- or two-sentence) answer to the question: Why are you a candidate? Your rationale should complete the statement "I am running for office because. . . . "

A convincing rationale will incorporate aspects of your personal, professional, and political biography that help to illustrate your reasons for running for office, what you hope to accomplish when in office, and the qualities that make you the best candidate for the office. For example, a candidate for school board might include the following rationale in her campaign message:

> As a parent of three, I've seen the facilities and quality of instruction at my children's schools go from good to bad to worse. I'm running for school board because I am motivated to restore a positive learning environment for our children and I have the ideas to get the job done.

This rationale explains how the candidate's experience as a parent has inspired her decision to run for office and informs what she hopes to accomplish once elected. Using your biography to explain your reasons for running is a good way to introduce yourself and your strengths to the voters and add credibility to your candidacy.

Choosing a Campaign Theme

A campaign theme serves as a bridge between the campaign rationale and the candidate's positions on policy issues. It is a phrase or sentence that makes your rationale for running for office relevant to the voters. Your campaign rationale answers the question: Why am I running for office? Your campaign theme answers the question: Why should voters care?

A campaign theme should be short and clear. It should be broad enough to encompass a wide range of issues and specific enough to be compelling to a voter who is not paying close attention to the election. It should also emphasize ideas with which most voters are familiar and with which they are likely to agree. For example, if you are running for a seat on the school board because you want to improve the quality of

---

■ BRIGHT IDEA: Ask Yourself the Important Questions

As you brainstorm what to include in your campaign message, here are some important questions to consider:

- What do I want to accomplish as a public official? Why is this important to me and why should it be important to the community?

- What are the key issues facing our community? Why are these issues important? What perspective do I bring to them? What ideas do I have for solving local problems?

- What's right about local government? What can be improved? What steps can be taken to make these improvements?

- What is my opponent likely to say about my qualifications for office and my positions on issues? What is my response?

- What key difficulties would I face if I won? How would I address them?

instruction and increase the resources provided by local schools, your
theme might be, "Improving our schools, investing in our future."

There are two sources of ideas for campaign themes: your stands on
key policy issues and your personal characteristics. Is the office to which
you are seeking election grappling with a major policy issue? Are there
major points of contrast between you and other candidates in terms of
leadership style, values, and experience? Anticipate the criticisms your
opponent(s) might make of you and turn these potential "negatives" into
positives. A lack of governmental experience, for example, may provide
"a fresh perspective" from an average citizen. The important point is that,
rather than listing your positions and experience, you develop a theme
that provides a succinct, relevant, and memorable summation of your
candidacy.

■ ADVICE FROM PROFESSIONALS: "Cutting Through the Noise," by Dan Schnur

The greatest competition that you will face in your campaign won't
come from your opponent. Your greatest challenge will be competing for
the attention of the voters.

You're not just competing against the other candidates in your race:
you're competing against every candidate for every office on the ballot.
You're competing with candidates for president and for governor, for
Congress and for the legislature. You're competing with candidates for
supervisor and for mayor, for city council and for school board, for county coroner and the mosquito abatement board. You're competing with
ballot initiatives and bond issues, and with every bit of political information available in this campaign season. And you're competing for the attention of an audience that doesn't care much for politics and politicians.

The competition doesn't stop there. War in the Middle East? Hur-
ricanes in the Gulf of Mexico? Juvenile crime in the inner city? Problems
with the space shuttle? They're all competing with your campaign for the
voters' attention.

And that's just hard news. If the local quarterback breaks his ankle,
if there's a new baby kangaroo at the zoo, if Jennifer Lopez has marriage

problems, you're competing with all of them, too. You're competing with HBO and professional wrestling and the Home Shopping Network. You're competing with chat rooms and home pages, with Nintendo and Napster.

Then there are jobs and families, car pools and Little League, Rotary, Kiwanis, and the PTA. Not to mention bills and chores and the million other things that fill up our lives every day.

Very few people are going to pay much attention to your campaign, and no one is going to care as much about your candidacy as you do. The reality is you're not going to get many chances to engage the voters: so when you do get their attention, you'd better be ready to take full advantage of the opportunity.

The best way to approach this challenge is to look at the voters' attention as a window. Most of the time, there are a lot of things going on outside that window for them to look at. Our goal is to get them to listen to you—even if just for a moment—and then to remember what they heard.

Some voters will never learn more about you than what they hear in this painfully short message summary. But if your message is sufficiently compelling, many people will want to learn more. Once you've lured them with that introduction, you can provide them the details of the issues, the goals, and the other priorities of your campaign.

In a nutshell, the easier your message is for voters to receive, the more likely it is they'll retain it. If the voters retain it, they're that much more likely to remember it. The more likely they are to remember your message, the more likely that they'll respond favorably to you when they get to the voting booth on Election Day.

Most people who know you will assume you're running for decent and honorable reasons. But most of the voters whose support you're seeking don't know you. To them, you're just another politician. (And we all know what people think of politicians, right?) Unless you explain to them the good reasons for your candidacy, they're going to assume the worst.

Hopefully, you are running because you believe you're better qualified to address the concerns of your community than others. Maybe you're running because you were inspired by Ronald Reagan or Bill Clinton, by Abraham Lincoln or Martin Luther King, Jr. Hopefully you're running because you think you can make a contribution that will make your community a better place to live.

No one knows that except for you, and unless you take the time to sit down and think through the reasons why you have decided to seek public office, you'll never be able to articulate those reasons to the voters. Until you take all those reasons and piece them together into a broader rationale for your candidacy, no one will be able to understand them. Here's the bottom line: unless you can summarize those reasons in a sentence or two, very few of those voters will stick around long enough to hear your explanation.

The most essential element of your rationale for candidacy is your own biography. Your biography—your life experiences—is what makes you the person you are. So it's important that voters who hear your rationale for candidacy learn something about you.

In a short one- or two-sentence rationale, you won't have the opportunity to tell the voters everything about your life history. What is important to tell them is the one thing that, more than any other, makes you who you are and makes you ready to lead.

Are you a parent? Maybe that has shaped your rationale for candidacy. Perhaps your profession has prepared you to run, and your experiences as a teacher or a farmer or a small businessperson provide the grounding for your rationale. Maybe you served in the military, or volunteered your time with welfare mothers, or heard a speech or sermon that inspired you.

As you build a broader message from your rationale, you can tell the voters other details about your life and your goals you think they need to know. In that rationale itself, make sure you find the one thing they need to know that will make them believe you when you tell them why you're running.

Many first-time candidates, worried about sounding vain or self-aggrandizing, are reluctant to talk about their accomplishments. Most of the time, you'll need to get past this reluctance. Remember this: no one will ever know these qualities in you unless you tell them.

It is only when you explain to them why that life experience helped make you the person you are today and how that experience developed the values that frame your life, that they can understand who you are and why they should be willing to support your candidacy.

Dan Schnur is a veteran of four presidential and four gubernatorial campaigns. He now teaches at the University of California, Berkeley and the Annenberg School for Communication at the University of Southern California.

Selecting Key Issues and Formulating Your Positions

Your campaign message should include your substantive positions on local issues or other matters of public policy that you want to address when you are elected. Because many voters have a limited attention span for and low level of interest in political campaigns, consultants typically recommend that you identify three policy issues that matter to the voters and to you and make these the focus of your campaign.

Consultants also recommend that you choose issues where you and most voters see eye to eye and where there is general agreement on their importance for the office that you are seeking. It is much more difficult and requires many more resources to change a voter's mind on an issue than it is to persuade an undecided voter to share your position or to emphasize an issue about which you and the voters already agree. You should develop positions on a broad range of issues in case voters ask you about them, but you should focus on three issues when you speak to voters and produce campaign materials.

Three criteria should guide your issue selection:

1. The issues that you choose must be important to you and to your candidacy. If you are not passionate about what you are speaking about people will know.
2. The issues you choose must be important to voters. Just because you think an issue is important does not mean voters will share your point of view.
3. Choose issues on which you and the voters you are trying to reach and mobilize agree.

You may want to keep in mind several other considerations when selecting issues:

- **Your issues should be broad enough to encompass the major duties of your office.**
  A candidate for city council with a background as a police officer, for example, may use her background to promote an agenda to reduce crime, but she should avoid being pegged as a one-issue candidate.

- **Your issues should fit with your rationale and theme.**
  If you run on a smart growth platform, your issue positions would address mixed use, transportation, and density concerns.

- **Select issues that you can discuss in depth and where you have ideas for improvement.**
  For each issue, it is important to feel comfortable elaborating on your ideas and answering a wide range of questions about your proposals.

- **Select issues where you can point to your relevant experiences or past successes.**
  This will add credibility to your positions.

- **Do not avoid issues that are a prime topic of discussion or concern.**
  Remember that your fellow candidates are selecting issues to focus on just as you are. If they focus on the issues that voters think are most important, so should you.

Communicating Your Ideas Effectively

Constructing your message is only the beginning of the process. You must communicate your message to voters, assess how it is being received, and hone your message delivery skills. Voters want substantive information, but they want it in an easily digestible format. As you start speaking to voters, follow these simple suggestions to make sure your message gets across:

- ### Be clear
  Your audience must understand what you are saying and what you are asking of them. Your message must be straightforward, follow logically, and be heard above all the "noise" in the lives of your listeners. Do not assume the audience already knows your message. State it in a

straightforward manner and respond to any hint that some listeners are not following your argument.

• Be focused

Your message must be laser sharp and should not attempt to convey too many things at once. It must speak to the interests and concerns of your audience. Voter attention spans are short and getting shorter. If you cannot fit your message into a few sentences, it may be lost. Candidates who seek to be comprehensive may overwhelm their audiences and cause them to remember nothing. Because people often remember more clearly the first and the last thing you say, repeat your key point in your conclusion to improve retention.

• Be compelling

Clarity and focus ensure that your audience understands your message, but whether or not they respond depends on how compelling your message is. Tell your audience not only what you want them to do but why they should do it. Whether your method of persuasion uses common sense and logic, current evidence and statistics, or appeals to core emotions and values, your message should compel the audience to care, to believe, and to act. Do not be afraid to speak from your heart but remember you are attempting to persuade others who may not share your assumptions and priorities. Articulate all of the reasons to support your candidacy, not

---

■ WHAT VOTERS WANT: Information on Issues and Candidates

To determine what types of information voters want from candidates, our survey of 2000 adult California residents asked respondents, "What are the top two things you are most interested in learning about the candidates: stands on issues, experience, character, intelligence, party platform, campaign practices, or something else?" The candidates' stands on issues was the clear favorite with 43%. "Character" was second with 26%, followed by experience (16%) and intelligence (8%). Very few respondents cited party platform (4%) or campaign practices (3%). When we asked focus group participants to describe what they dislike about campaigns, the lack of time and attention given by candidates to issues was a common refrain. Jeff said, "Instead of debating the actual issues, they're just trying to attack the individual for some personal experience that they might have had that isn't actually relevant to the job that they want to do, or the job that they will do."

Most focus group participants admitted that they are unlikely to read a candidate's position paper or even sit through a two-minute TV ad about the candidate. When asked if candidates should produce longer ads, many were skeptical that longer ads would be more informative (rather than simply longer attacks). Others bristled at the idea of being forced to watch anything longer than thirty seconds, even if the ad were more substantive. In general, while participants expressed a desire to learn more about the issues, it was clear that many do not want too many details, nor do they want to work too hard to get them.

merely those that underlie your opinions, and address potential counter-arguments.

BEST PRACTICE: Give voters the information they want.

If you are regularly asked certain questions about your background or local issues, your answers to those questions should be incorporated into your campaign message. If voters have other things on their minds when they hear from you, their focus will always override whatever you choose to focus on. If you directly address their questions and concerns, they will be more attentive listeners.

BEST PRACTICE: Make information about your candidacy easily available to voters.

Provide documentation for your qualifications and issue positions on your Web site and in your campaign materials, but don't make the text daunting and difficult to read. Present information with bullet points and headings and highlight important information in bold or italics. If someone requests information via email or phone or at their door, make sure that you respond quickly with the information they request.

Presenting Your Positions and Those of Your Opponent(s)

Voters want and need information to help them decide which candidate to support. Contrasting your positions and qualifications against those of your opponent(s) satisfies that need. On the other hand, voters react negatively to name-calling, character assassination, innuendo, and stereotyping. Using such techniques increases the risk of alienating voters. You can earn the respect of voters by demonstrating respect for your opponents even as you present voters with reasons to support you over other candidates.

Keep any criticism of your opponent(s) respectful, fair, relevant, and truthful. Despite the public's aversion to negative campaigning, research shows that voters are accepting of candidates who draw contrasts with other candidates' positions on key issues, especially when they provide independent documentation of their claims. If you present your own and your opponents' positions and qualifications truthfully, you will be more convincing when you make comparisons. Avoid half-truths or twisting the facts to create a false impression, as this can backfire when your opponent(s) or third parties respond.

Voters pay attention to the tone and timing of the contrasts that you draw, and you should too. Voters may interpret last-minute attacks that do not leave your opponent time to respond as an attempt to manipulate them. Creating a tone of civility among candidates leads to a more positive campaign. Voters are more accepting of comparative messages if they believe that the discussion is civil. The Golden Rule is relevant: if you do not want to be the object of negative campaigning by your opponent(s), avoid it yourself.

Some candidates choose to speak only of themselves, either because they believe that voters are averse to negative campaigning or because they believe it is unethical. You will need to determine the lines that you will not cross. However, refraining from contrasts can leave voters with little idea about what distinguishes you from other candidates (especially if your opponent is an incumbent). Political consultants advise candidates to provide voters with reasons why they are preferable to their opponents. If you choose not to draw contrasts, emphasize those qualities of your candidacy that distinguish you from the other candidate(s) in the race. If you are running against an incumbent, you can typically criticize current policies without making negative statements against him.

■ WHAT VOTERS WANT: Substance in a User-Friendly Format

Voters want substantive information about candidates, but they want it in a concise and accessible form. One focus group participant recommended that candidates use their ads to point voters to more information on their Web sites. The ad could "give a brief kind of positive message and say, 'If you'd like to learn more about this candidate, go to this Web site.' At the Web site, the campaign would present bullet points concerning where the candidate stands on the issues. You can go through whatever issues may seem pertinent to you, you can go there and check them out."

Members of another focus group proposed the idea of a "candidate résumé" as an objective and efficient way to learn about and evaluate candidates. The résumé would list the candidate's stands on issues, experience, qualifications, and other highlights of the candidate's biography, and would be widely distributed to voters. (A candidate might send his résumé to voters in the mail, drop it on voters' doorsteps, or post it on his campaign Web site.)

If you choose to draw contrasts, consultants advise that you find stark differences between your positions or qualifications and your opponent's. It is more difficult, for example, to emphasize slight differences on public spending than to point out that you favor a policy the other candidates oppose. When you do find areas of disagreement with your opponent(s), characterize your dispute truthfully. You may agree with your opponent's goals, for example, but not believe that she can achieve them with her proposal. Voters appreciate contrasts if they are stated as differences of opinion.

■ **BRIGHT IDEA: Be Careful in Drawing Contrasts with Your Opponent**

Before you criticize your opponent in public, ask yourself:

• Is it **truthful**? Can you document the truthfulness of your claims or the un-truthfulness of your opponent's?

• Is the subject of the attack **relevant** to the office for which you are running? Why or why not?

• Is it **fair**? Do your attacks or those of your opponent constitute half-truths that leave a false impression? Is the timing suspect?

You are more likely to get credit from voters, and be seen as credible, if you preface your critique with politeness. For example, if you disagree with a proposal made by your opponent, state that you want the campaign to be a discussion of proposals and you appreciate any that your opponent puts forward, even if you believe that this proposal is flawed. Or you might admit that there are positive aspects to your opponent's proposal but explain why the costs outweigh the benefits.

Voters appreciate your pointing out areas of agreement between you and your opponent(s), especially if your opponent is better known for her support of a particular issue on which you agree. You might preface the contrasts that you draw between you and your opponent(s) with an acknowledgment of where you agree.

There is likely to be information that voters want to learn about your opponents that your opponents are unlikely to provide. There is no shame in sharing that information if it is relevant to the election. Voters are tired of attack campaigns, however, and hold negative information to a higher standard. If you present it in the course of a primarily positive discussion about you, they are more likely to be accepting of it.

Contrasts are most effective when they highlight major differences that are obvious given factual information. For example, if you have experience that your opponent lacks or if you have developed a proposal for a solution to a problem that your opponent has ignored, pointing out these differences naturally follows from your emphasis on your own record and positions.

■ WHAT VOTERS WANT: Truthful, Relevant, and Fair Discussions of Candidate Differences

To assess public attitudes towards criticism in campaigns, our survey asked a balanced question about negative campaigning that would give voters reasons to oppose and support criticism between candidates:

> Some people say that in general, political candidates should never be critical of their opponents because campaigns have gotten too negative, while others say that candidates need to criticize their opponents because it is important to know the strengths and weaknesses of all candidates. Which of these comes closest to your view?

The question produced an evenly divided response, 51% said that the candidate should not criticize and 49% said they should.

Comments offered by focus group participants indicate that voters have a nuanced approach to criticism in campaigns, which may explain why half of the survey respondents said candidates need to criticize one another. Though focus group participants expressed their dislike for negativity in campaigns, they drew a distinction between acceptable criticism and unacceptable attacks. Some participants indicated a willingness to accept a negative campaign message if it provides useful information. In fact, many participants suggested that criticism is an acceptable and even necessary part of campaigns (for example, it is a candidate's responsibility to vet her opponent), as long as it is fair, relevant, and truthful.

Here is what voters considered to be **fair** criticisms:[1]

- A candidate who talks one way and votes another (71%).
- An opponent's voting record (68%).
- Not paying taxes on time (61%).
- Accepting contributions from special interest groups (57%).
- An opponent's business practices (53%).

The following examples voters perceive as unfair criticisms*:

- The actions of an opponent's family member (89%).
- Past personal financial problems (81%).
- Financing your campaign yourself (76%).
- Past troubles such as alcoholism or marijuana use (69%).
- Marital infidelity (57%).

---

[1] These findings are from a poll commissioned by the Institute for Global Ethics' Campaign Conduct Project and conducted by Lake Snell Perry & Assoc. and Deardourff/The Media Co. from June 6-11, 2002. Eight hundred likely voters were surveyed (sampling error is +/- 3.5%).

Protecting Yourself Against Attacks

No matter what kind of campaign you choose to wage, you can never control the actions of your fellow candidate(s). You have to be prepared for the likelihood that both your opponents and third parties will attack you during the course of the campaign. Research shows that ignoring these attacks or being unprepared for their arrival can be detrimental to your campaign. You should prepare the voters for any attacks that may be coming, do your best to answer the claims of your opponent(s) included in the attack, and bring the discussion back to your campaign message.

The best way to avoid a problematic attack is to release any negative information that your opponent may use against you yourself. It may sound counterproductive at first but political consultants advise that voters are less likely to react to a negative attack from your opponent if you have addressed it in advance. You should make a list of issue positions, aspects of your background, and potential scandals that your opponents may point to during the campaign.

■ **BEST PRACTICE:** Keep criticism relevant, truthful, and fair.

If you think that negative information is likely to come out, especially if it is available as part of the public record, you are better off getting it on the table prior to it being raised by your opponent. The media is less likely to consider the release of negative information about you news if you have already made an admission. Moreover, by releasing this information before your opponent does, you will have a chance to explain yourself or apologize for your actions before it appears to be politically expedient.

Sometimes you can use negative information about yourself to your advantage. You can argue, for example, that you have overcome a struggle in your past or that, like most voters, you are not perfect. If you have made a mistake, admit it forthrightly and tell voters what you have done to correct it and what you have learned from the experience.

Responding to Negative Claims

You cannot anticipate all negative attacks or inoculate yourself against all criticism. Be prepared to respond to negative information as it arises in your campaign. Political consultants recommend that you leave no attack unanswered. Provide as much information to counter an attack as quickly as possible. Issuing blanket denials is less effective than explaining how and why your record or proposals have been misinterpreted. Explanations are often complicated or cumbersome and it is your duty to make them as easy to understand as possible to the average voter.

Stating that the facts are complicated or referring people to elaborate documentation does not work as well as offering clear and simple explanations. Admit some fault where it is necessary and explain all distortions. As soon as an attack is made, you should enter a rapid-response mode of campaigning by releasing public statements and press releases. It may be helpful to demand that your opponent rescind an untruthful attack or ask the media to report that your opponent made an untrue accusation about you.

If you pledge to run a positive, issue-oriented campaign at the beginning of your campaign, this may help to discourage your opponent from launching negative attacks. The goal is to have such attacks look conspicuously discordant from the positive and informative tone that you are setting with your own campaign. Ask yourself if your opponent's attacks are truthful, relevant, and fair. Then do what you can to get the message out on why the attacks are untruthful, irrelevant, and unfair.

It is not at all clear that negative attack campaigning works. A 1998 study, for example, found that nearly half of the studies on political advertising show that positive advertising is more persuasive than negative advertising. Nearly a third of the studies found that negative

■ **WHAT VOTERS WANT: Contrasts Rather Than Personal Attacks.**

What are voters looking for in candidate communications? A 2002 survey* revealed:

- 88 percent think candidates should agree not to make any personal attacks.

- 78 percent think candidates should demand that outside groups pull unfair ads.

- 88 percent believe that candidates should refrain from using language or images that define other candidates based on their race, sex, or other personal characteristics.

*The poll was commissioned by the Institute for Global Ethics' Campaign Conduct Project and conducted by Lake Snell Perry & Assoc. and Deardourff/The Media Co. from June 6-11, 2002. Eight hundred likely voters were surveyed (sampling error is +/- 3.5%).

■ **BEST PRACTICE: Respond to attacks, but don't counterattack.**

advertising may backfire.[1] If you don't respond to negative attacks, however, voters may believe the information.

Whatever you do, resist the urge to respond in kind with an irrelevant counterattack. You run the risk that the counterattack will backfire, and you leave the original attack unanswered on the merits. If the attack is about an issue position, you may want to explain the true distinction between your position and your opponent's. State it as a simple contrast, however, so that you get credit for running a more civil campaign.

■ **LEARN MORE ON THE WEB:**

Use our contrast message worksheets to prepare for interactions with your opponent. We provide exercises with instructions to help you think through the likely contrasts between the candidates in your campaign. Learn more at campaigns.berkeley.edu.

If you have been attacked, voters are more willing to accept a response that draws a contrast between you and your opponent than they are if you initiate the confrontation. You do not want to get into a cycle of attack-counterattack, however. Make sure that your counter-statement contains all the relevant information on both sides of the dispute.

■ ADVICE FROM PROFESSIONALS: "The Perils and Pitfalls of Negative Campaigning," by Jonathan Wilcox

Given the widespread view that campaigns and elections are negative enterprises growing even more divisive over time, it may seem like quite a stretch to provide an entire thesis about the dangers, drawbacks, and difficulties associated with this political strategy.

But that's the point. The best political professionals know all about the powerful and delicate force that negative campaigning represents. The fact that they don't talk about it much says quite a bit about the strategic importance of knowing that they don't call it "negative" for nothing. Yes, people do respond to the negative—but they do so in two

---

[1] Brad Rourke, Wayne Saucier, and Matthew Krumme, *Clean Campaigns: How to Promote Candidate Codes of Conduct* (Institute for Global Ethics, 2001).

distinct ways. One can help you win a campaign. The other can help you lose it.

This is not to say that campaigns should be designed as Oxford Society debates governed by Robert's Rules of Order. Elections in America have always been rough and tumble contests that require skill as much as courage, decisiveness as much as devotion. That's never going to change, and it requires that political professionals serve up negative tactics like fine wine: never before its time.

Why is this? Because no aspect of campaigning is more widely misunderstood and consistently misused. Still, it remains the popular path of least resistance for many election efforts. The challenge is to know when to be clamorous *and* when to be contemplative. Remember: No one ever voted against any candidate because what he or she said or did was overly fair, considered, and balanced. This is that rare political virtue that can endure over literally decades of the dynamics of campaigns, issues, and personalities.

At the same time, the political cemeteries are lined with campaigns that, in thinking they were being tough and challenging, were instead obnoxious and unappetizing, giving voters little to vote for and plenty to vote against.

The contemporary political landscape provides three key reminders to consider when carefully evaluating the advantage of "going negative."

1. "Everything changed after . . . ."

If you work on only a few election contests, you are almost certain to meet him: the Campaign Commando. This individual seeks to inspire a political parallel with combat and the military arts, employing the jargon of the enlisted officer: Campaign tactics are "opening fire," "carpet-bombing," "utilizing guerilla warfare," "playing on enemy turf," and, for measured restraint, the occasional threat to "go nuclear."

But, as the cliché goes, everything changed after September 11.

Now that America is engaged in a real war, political strategists have wisely laid down some of their rhetorical arms. Those that haven't—and they are legion—risk using language that may inspire the campaign team, but offend the voters. Better to place the campaign effort in its rightful context: an important—even vital—contest of ideas and beliefs that will help determine our future course as a society. Campaigns are all those things; war, they are not.

2. Beware of D.O.G.

Almost every candidate shares a high-minded belief in seeking public office. They enter politics to make a difference, advance ideals, and
ensure a better future. Too often, this noble inspiration is left at the campaign door, and once inside, a playbook labeled "How to Win" guides
the election effort. A better way is to capitalize on the candidate's initial
impulse and let it guide and inform the cause.

This should not be seen as an invitation to a more righteous way of
living, but rather as a way to avoid the pitfalls of D.O.G.—Distracting
Our Guy. The inevitable urge to play hardball often takes a campaign in
a new and different direction, and the campaign morphs into a negative
enterprise.

Once a campaign goes into attack mode, it is compelled to involve
the candidate in ways large and small. Negative campaigning can then
become a diversion from the campaign's central purpose and alter its
course. The temptation for the candidate to take the lead in delivering a
negative message completes a transformation that many campaigns do
not intend.

3. It's not the blast, it's the fallout.

There's really only one place you don't want to be when a bomb
goes off: anywhere within the range of the explosion. Think of negative
campaigning this way: When a campaign strikes with a negative charge,
it means to do serious damage to the opposition. At least that's the plan.
But, get too close to your target, and the shock of the blast is sure to injure you, too.

Understood as an attempt to injure rather than inform, an attack is almost certain to backfire. The most effective negative tactics are informative rather than insulting, and it is imperative for great care and caution
to go into their execution. It's not as easy as slinging mud. That splatters,
too.

Consider this the negative campaign two-step: Land the blow, *and* be
out of range.

Conclusion

Negative campaigning is as old as campaigning itself. It's a legitimate tactic if done right, a potentially lethal one if done wrong. There is,
today, a certain romanticizing of the negative nature in campaigns, cred-

iting this or that charge with making the critical difference. This has happened, of course, but it almost always requires that the negative assault be part of the battle for a larger truth.

A negative campaign that meets the standard of a best practice is one that's based on facts, on real issues that satisfy the inherent common sense of voters. Seen in this light, maybe they're not so "negative" after all.

Jonathan Wilcox is an adjunct faculty member of the University of Southern California's Annenberg School for Communication and a former speechwriter for former California Governor Pete Wilson.

Ethical Promises and Codes of Campaign Conduct

One way to inoculate yourself against attacks and make voters aware that your campaign is different from those that have angered and alien-

---

■ WHAT VOTERS WANT: Pledge to Run an Ethical Campaign

Voters respond favorably to candidates who pledge to run ethical campaigns.

- 77% of the voters we surveyed said they would feel somewhat or much more favorably towards a candidate who signed a code of conduct pledging to "run a truthful, fair, and clean campaign."

- 71% said they would feel somewhat or much more favorably towards a candidate who signed a pledge to run an "issue-oriented campaign."

- 57% said they would feel somewhat or much more favorably towards a candidate who signed a pledge "not to use race, gender, religion, sexual orientation, or age as a basis for attacks."

Our focus group participants strongly supported codes of conduct. Some said that campaign codes would improve the tone and substance of a campaign by serving as a check on candidate behavior. For others, candidates who sign the code provide a valuable cue for assessing their candidacy. One participant said, "If a candidate signed something like this, then you'd look at that and say, 'That says something about him or her.' It helps you make a judgment about that person."

Our survey found that even pledging to avoid negative campaign behaviors is likely to elicit a favorable voter response. Of course, the key then is for the candidate to walk-the-talk of running a positive, issue-oriented campaign. By following through on your pledge, you demonstrate to the voters that you are a person who keeps his commitments, even when the going gets tough.

■ **BEST PRACTICE:**

Sign a code of conduct or make a public statement pledging to run a truthful, fair and clean campaign. Encourage your opponents to do the same.

■ **BRIGHT IDEA: Insulate Yourself From Potential Attacks**

The best way to ensure that you are not unfairly attacked is to acknowledge your weaknesses and "hang a lantern" on your problem. If you are open from the beginning about your weaknesses, you will get credit from voters for your honesty and reduce the effectiveness of attacks. One famous example is Ronald Reagan's statement in the Presidential Debates: "I promise not to make age an issue in this campaign. I will not hold my opponent's youth and inexperience against him." With humor, Reagan addressed the issue of his age, put it front and center, and made clear that any attack was unwarranted.

ated them in the past is to sign a code of conduct such as the Code of Fair Campaign Practices set forth in the California Elections Code, or make a public pledge to run an ethical campaign. These pledges help voters and the media keep you accountable and help you produce an image of responsibility.

You can set the tone of the campaign and make attacks less likely if you make such a statement and ask other candidates to follow suit. Your statement should include enforceable guidelines for what will be unacceptable, for example, forbidding attacks that are not about issues or qualifications. Ask the media to cover your and your fellow candidates' public pledge to run an ethical campaign and to follow up on whether you and your opponents have kept your promise.

The benefit of a written code is that you can establish enforcement criteria and make sure that all candidates are following the same rules of engagement. If you sign a code presented by a community organization, it can serve as a symbol of your commitment to engage in civil discourse.

Conclusion: Five Things to Know About Developing Your Message

1. Focus on your message.

To win, you will need to give voters a clear reason to support you. Presenting a list of your issue positions or accomplishments is not enough. Develop a clear, concise, and compelling message that serves as the centerpiece of your communications with voters.

2. Develop a rationale, a theme, and an issue focus.

Your campaign message should include three elements: (1) a rationale—your reason for pursuing office, (2) a theme—a succinct statement of why voters should support you that links your rationale to your issue positions, and (3) your positions on a few key policy issues that voters care about and on which you and the voters you want to mobilize agree.

3. Make your presentations simple and concise.

Design your message in a way that will appeal to voters who have scarce time and attention to give to your campaign. Focus on a few major points and present them clearly and repeatedly. Give voters a chance to learn more about you and your issues positions, but get them interested with simple and concise presentations.

4. "Hang a lantern on your problem."[2]

Inoculate yourself against attacks by alerting voters to your potential weaknesses before they become the subject of an attack. Explain your actions, apologize for past mistakes, describe how you have made amends, and tell voters what you have learned from the experience.

5. Leave no attack unanswered.

If your opponent attacks your record, proposals, or character, respond quickly with relevant information. Explain any inaccuracies or misinterpretations, admit any fault, and point out how the attack contrasts with your approach to campaigning.

---

[2] See Chris Matthews, *Hardball* (Simon & Schuster, 1988), chapter 10.

Funding Your Campaign

5

Money matters in politics. Financial resources are necessary for almost all campaign activities, especially advertising and organization building. (See Chapter 2 on developing a campaign budget.) Candidates with more financial resources can deliver their message to more voters more often. Success in fundraising is a signal to organizations, party leaders, and political reporters that you are a serious candidate.

As a candidate, you will be running an operation the size of a small business for several months. Unless you raise money, your organization will have no income. Saving money by using your home as your campaign headquarters and using volunteer labor may be good options for small races. But even if you do not plan to advertise or hire staff, the cost of materials can be steep.

Some candidates for local office attempt to campaign inexpensively and use their own funds. For some candidates, this may be a viable option. Too often, candidates underestimate the costs of campaigning, attempt to raise money when it is too late, and incur major debt in their effort to win. No matter what your expected level of expenses, you should develop a realistic budget and a fundraising strategy that allows you to raise the necessary funds in a timely fashion and avoid going into debt.

Planning Your Fundraising Strategy

Deciding to raise money puts you in the game. To succeed, you need to plan your strategy and focus your energy on achieving your goals. This requires budgeting, brainstorming, and a willingness to pursue many leads even if most are unsuccessful. Candidates will raise more money if they plan carefully, take a prominent role in their own fundraising, and recruit a group of supporters to help.

It Starts with a Plan

Fundraising is too important to leave to happenstance. Effective and successful fundraising requires a plan, based on a campaign budget and a timeline that specifies when amounts of money must be raised to meet cash flow requirements. The goal should be to keep ahead of your expected expenses so that you always have some cash on hand. If you do not meet your fundraising goals, you can always adjust them, but if you don't have a plan you will never know what your fundraising goals should be.

One quick way to estimate the cost of your campaign is to check the campaign finance reports of those who have campaigned in the past for the office you are seeking, especially those who won. Remember, campaign costs go up in every cycle due to inflation and political trends. If you are trying to estimate your own expenses, always budget more than you initially think you will need. If you plan to advertise, check rates in advance.

> ■ **TAKE NOTE:**
>
> Raise funds in advance of expenses—not as they occur—so you always have some cash on hand.

If you plan to rent office space, research its likely cost. If you plan to hire staff, think about how many employees you will need and estimate the wages you will need to pay them.

Your fundraising plan should be more than a list of prospective donors and a budget. It should include the methods you will use to raise the money your campaign needs, such as fundraising letters, phone lists, online donations, and events. A diverse fundraising effort gives you the opportunity to ask for and receive donations from all types of contributors —from a house party attendee to an official political committee.

■ ADVICE FROM PROFESSIONALS: "The Money Hunt: Drafting a Fundraising Plan," by Joanne Davis

You don't have to plan to fail; all you have to do is fail to plan.
Unknown

Does having a finance plan mean that your campaign will be guaranteed the money you need to win? No, but having a plan and following it will ensure that your fundraising operation is organized, efficient and able to maximize all fundraising opportunities. *That* will get you the funds you need.

Ideally, a candidate should not head the fundraising operation. If you have the resources, hire a professional fundraiser. If not, ask a trusted friend who is goal-oriented, has good management and organizational skills, and is attentive to detail to be your finance director.

Then make sure he or she understands that any good fundraiser can go out and raise money. But a good fundraiser, working with a good finance director, can really maximize the dollars that will flow into a campaign. If you serve as both fundraiser and finance director, it is imperative that you combine the strategy of planning the finance program with the implementation skills needed to execute the plan.

Many people abhor planning. There are 10,000 excuses folks come up with—planning takes time, planning takes strategic thinking, planning demands the use of systems and time management. Many campaigns lurch forward at their inception without a thought to developing a fundraising plan—or they hire a fundraising consultant and expect dollars to miraculously start flowing into the bank account. Sometimes it works and money is raised; yet without a plan you may miss important sources of contributions and fail to build relationships with donors that will ensure consistent fundraising in the future.

Building a finance plan is really not that complicated. The challenge is to make sure that the finance organization is well integrated with the rest of the campaign. Don't let the finance operation stand alone—those charged with raising money must know what the communications, polling, scheduling, and political arms of the campaign are doing in order to maximize fundraising.

After it has been established and confirmed by the candidate and the campaign manager that fundraising and finance are interrelated with every aspect of the campaign, the fundraiser and finance director (if there is one) should write a plan. Key to that plan are the following elements:

- ### Identify the amount to be raised.
Sounds obvious, but you must have a clear understanding of what the candidate and the campaign management team are expecting to spend before you can write a plan. Question the amount needed—has the amount been calculated after careful examination of the race? If you believe so, then you are ready to discuss honestly whether or not it is an achievable goal. You must also be able to confidently promise donors that their investment will be wisely managed—you have a fiduciary responsibility to the donors as well as the candidate that the money will be properly managed.

- Identify the team that is going to raise the money.

If you are fortunate enough to have a Finance Chairman, a person who will lead the finance committee, work with that individual to draw up the plan and make certain that he or she is committed to help with the fundraising efforts.

From there, develop a committee. Ask each member to take responsibility for raising a specific amount of money. Make them accountable and make sure they are working. Give them the support they need and stay in constant communication with them. The candidate must be willing to acknowledge the committee's efforts as well, with public acknowledgement and private thanks.

- Assemble a list of every possible source of funds.

If you are working with a new candidate, you will no doubt start with that individual's holiday card list, then move on to his or her colleagues, neighbors, friends, and business associates.

Even if you are working for a candidate who already has a "housefile" of donors, you must constantly be researching possible new donors. The Internet is a treasure chest of information—you can look up donors to nonprofit organizations, other candidates, political parties, ideological causes, etc. Note: federal law prohibits the use of federal campaign reports for the purpose of soliciting contributions. The possibilities are endless, but you must incorporate this "prospecting" into your overall finance plan.

- Incorporate all methods of fundraising into your plan.

There are many methods of fundraising, some generate more contributions than others. They should all be part of your plan. Common methods include events, telephone calls, telemarketing, web contributions, donor clubs with member benefits, and direct mail. The challenge is to *go beyond the common methods!* What else is out there that can be incorporated into the finance plan in order to generate funds? A great example is Howard Dean's use of Internet-based fundraising to generate income for his presidential primary campaign. It's this kind of effort that will make your finance plan the envy of everyone—including your opponent! Set up a Web site where donors can give directly (on-line) to your campaign. Include your Web site address in all your campaign materials.

- ## Use tools provided by other arms of the campaign organization.

This is where the integration of the finance operation with the entire campaign organization is vital. Know the political direction that the campaign is taking so that you can more appropriately target donors—for example, by ideology. Use all of the endorsements that the political team has secured in order to bring credibility to the campaign. While you can never guarantee a win, donors like to know that the campaign is viable—endorsements will reassure them. Feed polling data (if you have it) to donors and potential donors to let them know how the campaign is going and encourage more contributions. Work with the communications team to know the talking points and distribute them to your donors—they will really feel a part of the campaign with this information. Work with the scheduler to make sure that the candidate has time for fundraising calls or will remember to show up at the fundraising events you plan.

- ## Set up a tracking system to track contributions.

You must be able to tell how much money has come in, from what events, and what else is out there. At any given time the campaign management team is going to want to know how much they can spend. If you set up a comprehensive tracking system, you will be able to supply that information at the touch of a computer key.

- ## Don't forget to say thank you—and ask again!

A simple thank you letter and/or phone call is imperative to the success of your efforts. Donors want to know that the candidate and the campaign recognize their contribution, no matter what the level. So, someone who gives $25, and receives a postcard thank you promptly, is much more likely to contribute another $25. A donor who gives a maximum contribution and receives a personal thank you letter is much more likely to go out and recruit others to give the maximum than a donor who gives and is never recognized. Unless the campaign is so well funded that it doesn't need any money, each thank you should include a line inviting the donor to participate further—either by recruiting others to give or to give again themselves.

A good finance director is not necessarily a good fundraiser, and vice versa. Building a strong finance plan and putting the systems in place to implement the plan will enable the fundraisers to work more efficiently and effectively—*and raise more money!*

Joanne Davis is president of The Davis Group and has over twenty years of experience overseeing the fundraising efforts of top elected officials, state political parties, and nonprofit organizations in California and nationwide.

Creating a Finance Committee

A diverse group of supporters that help raise funds will expand the number of potential donor prospects for the campaign. Finding a campaign treasurer is the first step; the second is to appoint a fundraising director to oversee the development and implementation of the fundraising plan.

Next, form a finance committee of people with a large pool of friends and acquaintances to ask for money. Committee members can use their contacts to set up meetings with prospective donors; they can host fundraising events and get others to do so. Pick committee members with different contacts, rather than your closest friends and work colleagues. You want your committee to cast its net as wide as possible.

The joint nature of the enterprise creates mutual accountability and even a little friendly competition. Periodic reports (by email) and meetings to assess progress will keep the effort on track. Committee members can allocate calls to prospective donors among themselves and make decisions about prospects that the candidate should contact. Such meetings are an opportunity for the candidate to express appreciation for what committee members are doing.

Identifying Your Donors and Developing a Target List

Raising money is based on a simple principle: contributions require contributors and larger numbers of contributors produce more contributions. As you brainstorm, write down specific names along with categories of potential contributors, such as members of community groups or clients. As your list grows, your donations should grow exponentially because every contributor can help convince others to contribute.

Whom to Ask?

Your friends, family, coworkers, professional associates, members of groups to which you belong, those who contributed to previous campaigns of like-minded candidates, and those who support your positions on the issues (or strongly oppose your opponents' positions) are all po-

> ■ **TAKE NOTE:**
>
> The people who are most likely to contribute are those who have contributed before.

tential donors to your campaign. Prepare a list of potential donors, their contact information, their previous giving history, and people on the campaign who know them. Call those most likely to give first, but contact *everyone* on the list.

Some candidates believe that once someone has donated to a campaign, he or she has contributed his or her due and should be crossed off the list. This is directly contradicted by professional advice, which says that those who are most likely to contribute are those who have contributed before. In other words, if someone donates to the campaign, he or she should become a target of future fundraising, not taken off the list.

Tactics for Soliciting Large and Small Donations

Large donations are typically acquired through direct contact with the candidate or someone in the candidate's inner circle. As you develop your list of names, make sure that you indicate the range of likely contributions from each person. Supporters with higher incomes, more interest in politics, a history of political donations, and more stake in the outcome of the election are all more likely to be large donors. Candidates should make personal phone calls to everyone they know in the large donor category, unless the potential donor is a close friend of someone working on the campaign.

If large donors are noncommittal, tell them that you will call back after they have had a chance to think it over. If they say they will donate later, follow-up with phone calls and send donation envelopes. If their friends have contributed, mention that they are supporters. If someone gave you his or her name as a potential contributor, prominently mention your contact and why they thought the prospect would contribute.

Small donations are usually made in the form of checks written at fundraising events and in response to fundraising letters. Sources of potential fundraising lists include donors to similar past candidates and organizational mailing lists. Small donors still like to feel connected to the candidate so do anything you can to personalize your letters.

When planning your events, appoint different people to oversee them, select locations all over your district, and tell everyone to invite their friends. Appeals to small donors should include a statement of the stakes of the election, an indication that the campaign is on track but needs more help to win, and easy methods of contributing.

If people cannot offer financial assistance, give them a list of other ways they can help the campaign (placing a sign in their yard, making phone calls, walking door-to-door, etc.). You can accept in-kind contributions, subject to any applicable contribution limits, such as office supplies and advertising, which can help to reduce expenses to the campaign.

Fundraising Tools: Phone Calls, Direct Mail, and Events

The primary methods of fundraising are face-to-face meetings, phone calls, letters, and events. Each requires a different set of skills and type of preparation but all are critical to your fundraising success. In general, face-to-face meetings and candidate phone calls should be reserved for large donors; letters and phone calls from supporters should be used for small donations, though large donations should always be requested. All supporters should be invited to your events.

Writing an Effective Fundraising Letter

The core of any direct mail package to your supporters should be a fundraising letter. As with all of your campaign materials, the most important aspect of the letter should be clear prose that makes reading easy. Use bullet points, headings, bold, and italics liberally but not in a way that makes the piece difficult to read. Personalize your letters. Use names in the address and greeting and then use "you" and "I" throughout the letter.

Your letter should say that the campaign is going well but needs more resources to keep the momentum going. Emphasize the need for immediate contributions; inform the reader that a contribution is more valuable if it arrives earlier rather than later in the campaign. Stress the benefits that supporting your candidacy will bring (for example, by helping ensure the election of a person with values or issue positions similar to those of the letter's recipient). Avoid, of course, any implication that support for your candidacy will result in any special favors or access.

Do not be afraid to repeatedly ask for contributions in the letter. Ask for a specific amount or range of contributions, but leave open the option of a lower amount. Include a request for "in-kind" contributions, such as, free printing services, office space, refreshments for volunteers, and other tangible gifts that might benefit the campaign.

■ **LEARN MORE ON THE WEB:**

See our sample letters and event invitations at campaigns.berkeley.edu.

Keep in mind that your base may require a slightly different message than swing voters. Tailor your letter to your audience and to the political context. Comparisons with your opponent(s) are still helpful, even if you know that the recipient is a solid supporter. To make your letter current, you might include references to popular culture or recent events that have been in the local news. Before printing and sending out your letters, test them out on friends and campaign volunteers and ask them to suggest improvements.

■ **BRIGHT IDEA: Online Contribution Forms**

On your Web site, make it possible—and easy—to contribute. Include a form so you can contact prospective donors by phone. You can use third party services to accept credit card contributions (for a fee).

Other materials should accompany your letter in the direct mail package. Make sure to include a matching reply card and envelope. Request contact information, including email and phone numbers, on the card. Provide an opportunity for people to offer other help, including volunteering, hosting an event, and displaying a yard sign. In the package, a personalized letter should be the first thing the recipient sees. Do not be discouraged by a small response rate to your direct mail fundraising efforts. It can cost up to forty cents for every dollar you raise using direct mail.

Planning Fundraising Events and House Parties

The key to a successful fundraising event is to keep it simple and minimize costs. Do not limit yourself to either big- or small-ticket events; a variety will enable you to appeal to a broad spectrum of the donor community. Start planning early and ask many people to host events. Individuals can host house parties and committee members can host public events. Put the names of your hosts on all materials, including invitations. If your event requires tickets, recruit lots of people to sell tickets. Consultants estimate that each ticket seller will only sell about five tickets for each event.

Select locations that are accessible and well known to your supporters. Do not underestimate the value of an intriguing location or activity. (An example might be a newly renovated historic home.) This helps to attract participants and encourages people to show up. Inviting local celebrities or other special guests to your events can improve attendance.

> ■ **BRIGHT IDEA: Fundraising Envelopes**
>
> Include fundraising envelopes in campaign mail and carry them with you to distribute to new supporters you meet on the campaign trail.

At the event, your primary concerns will be seating and space. Make sure that you have room for everyone but that the room does not appear empty. If the event is private, make the participants feel involved in the campaign by updating them on recent and future events.

Contribution cards and envelopes should be abundantly available throughout your campaign. They should be preprinted with the campaign's address and include all the information required by state and local campaign reporting laws. Envelopes should be included in campaign mailings and carried by the candidate and volunteers to all events.

Meeting with Prospective Donors

The best way to generate high dollar contributions is to meet face-to-face with potential contributors. This approach to fundraising must go hand in hand with other efforts. Make a phone call to set up these meetings and send campaign materials before you meet. Some meetings will be impromptu, perhaps occurring at an event. No matter what the circumstances, be prepared with a pitch and contribution materials.

At your meetings, try to establish a rapport with your prospect quickly and move to your pitch. It is helpful to make your donors feel connected to you and to your campaign, but this should not distract you from asking for money. Your pitch should include your rationale for running and a brief statement of what you hope to accomplish as an officeholder, but most of it should emphasize your common ideas and interests with the prospective donor. This means you will need to prepare for the meeting by obtaining and reviewing information on the donor's background and major issue concerns. Make your donors feel they are part of your inner circle, but do not tell them they will receive special favors for their contribution.

The most important part of the conversation is when you ask the person to contribute a specific dollar amount. Afterwards, pause and be patient. Let your donors ask questions and voice their concerns, but make it clear that you would like a check from them before you leave. The most common excuse given by donors is that they cannot afford to make a contribution. You can respond by offering to accept a lesser dollar amount and by pointing out that you are most interested in their financial support, rather than the specific amount.

Be prepared to answer your prospective donors' questions. Most will want to know about your chances of winning. They may ask how much money you have already raised, who is helping you with the campaign, what groups have endorsed you, and what your plan is to win the election. You should have good answers to these questions and be armed with the latest indications that your campaign is gaining momentum.

If your prospects offer to contribute, ask them to give you a check at that time and make sure you gather the required information. Request names of other potential contributors and ask permission to use their names in your solicitations.

■ ADVICE FROM PROFESSIONALS: "Asking for Money," by Michelle Maravich

Dear Abby,

I am thinking of running for political office. Where should I begin? Every time I think of having to raise money to support my candidacy, my palms get clammy, my heart starts racing, my throat goes dry and I want to quit! What should I do?

Signed,

Wanna B. Elected!

Dear Wanna B.,

You are not alone. Many who have gone before you have suffered the same stage fright. Here are a few ideas to help you launch your fund-raising ship:

Tip one: Hire a stunt double.
Tip two: Self-finance.
Tips three, four and five: Mortgage your house, marry rich,
 hit the lottery.

If these tips are not helpful, then try this: sit down, get organized, and dive in. Virtually every candidate has to raise money for his campaign, and it is an important test of both the candidate's viability and commitment to his candidacy. Convincing voters that you are the right choice at the ballot box starts with convincing your friends and others that you are an important investment and that your message deserves to be heard.

Here's an outline of steps to follow when fundraising:

Step One: Identify donors and rank your list.

Whether this is a first time candidacy or a re-election, the overall process of raising funds remains the same. Begin by identifying donors out of your sphere of influence and ranking the approach and amount of money to be asked.

Identifying: The candidate compiles a list of potential donors, including everyone she knows—friends, family, business associates; the names of past donors (if they exist) or people who have contributed to candidates for this office in the past (ask previous candidates for a list of names, you can also get this information from the government entity that regulates your election); and the names of donors who should care (business, labor, PACs). As the campaign progresses, the list will grow.

Ranking: After compiling your list of donors, rank them by their ability to contribute, propensity to contribute, and the fundraising tool to reach them. The candidate and the finance team do this task. I use a coding system of letters and numbers. The letters (A-D) define the proximity of the potential donor to the candidate, with "A" being those closest to the candidate and "D" being those furthest away. Next to the letter, place a number indicating the amount the potential contributor will be asked to give. For example, a potential contributor could be assigned an A/100, reflecting his close relationship with the candidate and his ability to contribute $100. Another potential contributor could be assigned a C/2500, reflecting a business relationship in the district and her ability to contribute $2,500. While this system is subjective and based upon the judgment calls of the candidate and staff, it provides a structure and a road map for the candidate calls and solicitations.

Step Two: Develop your strategy.

Begin your fundraising by calling the "A" donors with the highest dollar level. Once you finish the As, move on to the Bs and work your way down the list. I recommend candidates call all the way through the D names. Everyone must be asked to support your campaign and the best way to do this is through a direct and personal call.

Each group of donors requires a different approach and different expectations. If there are people on your list whom you feel would be able to solicit their friends, ask them to host a fundraising event in addition to giving to your campaign. As you work into the Cs and Ds, some of these people will need to meet with you before giving to your campaign, since they are further from your sphere of influence. Leaders of PACs and other interest groups may ask for a meeting with you or ask you to interview with members of their organization to see if you merit their support. Remember that everyone needs a call to start the process. It is important to prepare a letter of introduction about your candidacy and campaign to send to potential donors if requested.

Once your campaign has organized fundraising events, invite potential donors to attend these events when you call them, but remember that events are only vehicles to collect the money. Try to get a financial commitment from them at the time you place the call.

Keep your list clean and well organized. Make sure all donor contact information is up to date. Keep all names on the list, even those who indicate they will not be supporting your campaign, and provide a space for making notes about each prospect. You or your staff may need to be reminded of whether a potential donor declined to make a contribution later in the campaign or the next time you run. It is important to keep accurate, long-term records—someone who says no to you the first time you run may support you later as you move to higher office.

While you may have already placed calls to and even collected contributions from some of the people on your list, be sure to invite everyone on your list to your fundraising events since it provides an opportunity for them to see you and see the momentum of your campaign. They may be inspired to increase their contribution!

Step Three: Develop a compelling message.

Before you ask for money, develop your basic political and fundraising messages and understand how, when, and why they are used. You must be able to answer these questions:

1. Why are you running for office?
2. What is your personal history? Why are you qualified for this office?
3. Who is supporting you? What individuals, organizations, business leaders, and other notable people have already given money, endorsed your campaign, and offered other forms of support?
4. Why should someone support you?
5. How much money do you need to win?

Donors, like investors, need to know how much money is needed and why. All the primary players (the candidate, steering committee, and staff) must know and be able to clearly state exactly what the success of this campaign means and how much money it is going to take to win.

■ **Tips for meeting with prospective donors:**

• Do not be late.
• Be optimistic.
• Be aggressive.
• Be sincere.
• Be enthusiastic.
• Be convincing.
• Be flexible.
• Do not lie or mislead.
• Stay away from volatile issues.
• Do not take the prospect or their money for granted.
• Don't leave without a check.
• Ask for names of other potential contributors.

Step Four: Ask for money.

Whether you are asking for money in person or over the phone, follow these guidelines:

1. Establish a rapport. Acknowledge who they are and how you know them or why they should be interested in giving to you.
2. Tell them how they will benefit from your election.
3. Demonstrate how you can win. (Cite recent poll numbers, a weak challenger, money in the bank, significant endorsements or any other evidence that proves the viability of your candidacy.)
4. Tell them how their contribution will be used.
5. Ask for a specific amount.
6. Shut up! Wait for their response before you say another word. Give them the opportunity to think through the request and let them respond. They may surprise you with a yes and a larger amount than you expect. If they agree to give, make arrangements to immediately collect their contribution. If they say no, find out why—perhaps the timing is not right for them.
7. Once you have received their contribution, immediately send a thank you! If it is a large contribution, you may want to call and thank them.

Remember, if you don't ask, people won't give.
The corollary to this rule is: What is the worst that could happen?

Here's what I post for every candidate:
Long phone calls mean fewer phone calls.

Always ask for dough.

If you don't ask, people won't give.

Just because they won't give, doesn't mean they don't like you.

Leadership takes time, time is money, money is scarce and that's not funny.

Time is limited, fundraising is hard work, life is short, and campaigns are shorter.

Now show me the money!

Michelle Maravich has led the fundraising efforts for the California Democratic Party and the California Coordinated Campaign for the past five years and is one of California's leading political fundraisers.

■ **BRIGHT IDEA: Role Playing**

If you or your volunteers are new to fundraising or are uncomfortable asking for money, run through some mock meetings or phone calls with potential donors. Develop an outline of key points to be made, including:

• The campaign's key messages
• Respected organizations or individuals who have endorsed or contributed to the candidate
• What kinds of campaign activities the donation will support (based on the campaign budget)
• The amount being requested
• A request for names of others who might contribute

Materials to take to a meeting include the campaign plan and budget, the candidate's biography and positions on key issues, and pledge envelopes with blanks for the required campaign reporting information.

■ ADVICE FROM THE FRONT LINES: "Why I Donate to Political Campaigns," by Shaun R. Lumachi

When I believe in candidates and their political views I donate to their campaigns. There are also times when I disagree with candidates on specific policies, but still make a donation based upon our friendship and my belief in them as a person.

I have a friend who recently won a seat on his hometown city council. Our friendship began in college when we worked together in student government. We sometimes found that we disagreed, philosophically, on policy related issues that impacted the people that we represented. However, he has gained my support through experiences we have had as friends.

I respect his ability to seek advice from people in his decision-making process. He is confident about his ability to make good decisions and is not afraid to fail. As a leader, he focuses on goals and works hard for results. We have these characteristics in common. His city council election was important to me because I wanted to see my friend, a person I strongly believe in, succeed in fulfilling his goal of being a public servant.

I will also donate to a political campaign when I do not know the candidate but believe in his or her policies. I am an advocate for our state's business community. I support policy issues that enable our community to flourish by creating more jobs. I recently donated to a candidate running for the California state legislature who shares my views. I have a desire to see him win because he will apply our shared philosophies when voting for laws that impact my community. He believes in opposing new taxes. The current political climate in our state assembly is heating up when it comes to supporting taxes. Numerous laws have been proposed that would raise taxes and impose new ones to deal with our state's budget deficit. I believe increasing taxes will deter business growth in our state. Electing representatives who will oppose new taxes is vital to the success of our businesses and creating more jobs for our citizenry.

My belief in the person and his ability to succeed is important in my decision to donate to his political campaign. Working closely with my friend in college enabled me to establish a relationship and learn more about him. Through active participation in local government I was able to donate to a candidate who shared my views on certain policies. Building relationships and participating in the political process are the two key factors that influence my support for candidates.

Shaun R. Lumachi is a community leader and president of Chamber Advocacy, a professional advocacy consulting firm that empowers chamber of commerce members by showing them how to leverage their voices in public policy discussions and decision making.

Soliciting Support from Constituency Groups

You can accept support from groups as well as individuals. The benefit of group contributions is that they tend to be larger and can serve as jumping off points for other contributions from group members. As you develop your target list, make sure you consider including all local groups that contribute to local candidates as well as groups you belong to that might consider supporting you.

Some groups may be prohibited by their internal rules or campaign finance regulations from contributing directly to your campaign. These groups still may provide fertile ground for individual contributions and you should solicit invitations to speak to their members.

Not All Support is Helpful

When meeting with constituency groups or individuals, make clear that what a contributor is supporting is a person who will always exercise his or her best judgment about what is best for the community—someone who will serve the public with integrity and conscientiousness. If you get the sense a potential donor is expecting a specific return on his investment in your candidacy, be clear that your expectations are different. If he continues to imply that he wants something for his contribution, point out that the law does not allow you to make such promises and you cannot accept the contribution unless he understands that it will not buy him anything but an ethical public official.

What about contributions from adult business owners, developers with project applications pending, or others who might reflect poorly on the candidate and the campaign? Voters are suspicious of a candidate whose campaign appears to have been bankrolled by those who have a direct stake in the candidate's future decisions as an elected official. Moreover, your opponents may make an issue of such support in the campaign in an effort to undermine the voters' trust in you. This is where "good ethics is good politics." Although such contributions may look like easy money, accepting them may cause more headaches for the campaign in the long run.

> ■ **BEST PRACTICE: Be clear about the lack of quid pro quo.**
>
> Do not give contributors the impression that you will do something as an officeholder in exchange for their contribution. If you think they are expecting this kind of treatment, be up front about how your expectations do not match theirs.

Disclosing Contributions Made to Your Campaign

If you do not feel comfortable telling people about who is contributing to your campaign, you are probably soliciting contributions from the wrong types of supporters. Public disclosure will be requested by the media and may be required by law. Since the information is often public already, you should make it as accessible as possible, for example, by prominently displaying the names of your contributors on your Web site. Talk to reporters and voters about the contributions you have received from many small donors and community organizations to illustrate the depth and breadth of support for your candidacy.

If you release more information than the law requires, you can point out your openness to the voters and members of the news media and ask your opponents to be just as open as you. This is especially helpful if you believe that you are being more conscientious than your fellow candidate(s) in deciding whom to ask for contributions. In all campaigns, disclosure can serve as a signal to voters of your integrity.

■ **WHAT DO VOTERS WANT?:**
Disclosure of Campaign
Contributors

Our survey found that voters favor candidates who disclose information about their campaign contributors. The survey asked, "If a candidate publicly released a list of his campaign contributors and amounts received as soon as he got them, would this make you view him much more favorably, somewhat more favorably, or would it make no difference to you?" Forty percent of respondents answered "much more favorably," and 26 percent said "somewhat more favorably." (Thirty percent said it would make no difference.) On a scale of 1 to 3 (where 1 = "no difference," 2 = "somewhat more favorably," and 3 = "much more favorably") the average response was 2.13.

Focus group participants expressed a similar degree of support for candidates who disclose their contributors. Participants noted the symbolic power of disclosure: by making information about their contributors easily accessible to the public, candidates add transparency to their campaigns and demonstrate that they don't have anything to hide.

Conclusion: Five Things to Know about Financing Your Campaign

1. No one will give unless asked.

A veteran congressional fundraiser observed that the effective fundraiser is one who will ask ten more people for money after having asked ten people for money and having been turned down by nine. Knowing what donors have given to other candidates can help you decide how much to ask for. Some professionals recommend going twenty percent above what one might reasonably expect a donor to give based on past history; the donor will sometimes give somewhere between past amounts and the amount requested.

2. The candidate is the most effective fundraiser.

Most large contributors expect a direct appeal from the candidate, usually in person. You can ask your supporters to identify and introduce you to likely contributors, but you should always be directly involved in soliciting large donors. Be prepared to make the sale with information and answers to common questions.

3. Do not exchange contributions for political favors.

> ■ **BEST PRACTICE:** Disclose campaign contributions.
>
> Keep records of your contributors and their contributions and make this information public. Practice disclosure to build your reputation as an open and ethical public servant.

The last thing you want is for a contributor to think that his or her contribution controls your decision making, even on a single issue, once you are elected. Your duty as an elected official is to act in the best interest of the community and not to provide special favors to your contributors. Make your expectations clear to donors who may have different ideas about what their contribution will buy.

4. In-kind contributions can be as valuable as money.

Every donated item represents money you do not have to spend and is just as good as the equivalent money raised. As you plan your campaign budget, for each expense item ask whether someone might be in a position to donate it.

5. Thank your contributors.

Acknowledge every contribution, however modest, immediately. It is not just a courtesy; thanking your contributors is a relationship-building tool that keeps the door open for future requests for assistance. Create a system to make sure donors are always thanked in a timely fashion.

Delivering Your Message

6

Finding the right message is only part of the process of convincing voters to vote for you. To win, you will need to deliver your message effectively using free and paid media and opportunities to speak in public venues. You cannot speak to every voter. Take advantage of community resources that allow you to speak to large crowds and broadcast your message across your constituency.

The Benefits of Free (or "Earned") Media

Successful candidates know how to use the media to amplify their message without spending all of their resources on advertising. "Free media" is a term used to indicate media coverage of your campaign that is not purchased, such as appearances on radio or television or an article in the newspaper. These appearances typically arise in the course of news coverage about the campaign. In contrast to the old adage "all publicity is good publicity," candidates must be attentive to their news coverage and act to mold it in a way that is informative to voters and helpful to the campaign's goal of getting its message out.

Free media is often called "earned media" by professionals to emphasize that despite its lack of a price tag, it does not come easy. The media typically give sparse coverage to local politics and that coverage is divided among candidates. The coverage that they do provide is often "horse-race" analysis: they tell who is likely to win but do not provide information that voters can use to decide who they should support. When members of the news media do cover the candidates' qualifications and issue positions, they often cover "he said—she said" disputes among the candidates or mention that one candidate is accused in a scandal.

To get the kind of coverage you want, be proactive in your solicitation of media coverage. When reporters do cover you, be prepared to make statements that will appear in the news and bring your message to voters. This requires strategic action, persistence, and preparedness. Working with the media is a central task of a campaign.

Free Media Strategies

The first rule of gaining free media is to make it easy for local media outlets to reach you. You should identify all of the local media outlets that might cover your race and make sure that they have the campaign's telephone number and email address and that someone is assigned to respond promptly to their requests. If a reporter wants to speak to you, respond as quickly as possible and volunteer to sit down for a face-to-face or telephone interview. If you develop a reputation as someone who is easily accessible, reporters may want to do stories on your campaign and may call you for comment when they are covering other political stories.

To generate media coverage, however, you will need to do more than sit back and wait for the phone to ring. Act to create news. Put yourself in a reporter's position and ask what might be newsworthy about your campaign. The media are generally interested in whatever might interest a large number of voters, but they usually only cover events—things that they can say happened today—rather than ongoing policy discussions. When you hold events or issue public statements, try to think of the media angle or "hook." Ask yourself these questions: What kind of story might be written about the event? Why is it interesting and who might cover it?

Be inventive about creating news. You will not always get an opportunity to deliver your complete and unedited message in the news but you may find ways to highlight your issue stances or the support you have received by piggybacking on other news events. When you are planning events, know the news cycle and take advantage of slow news days to attract coverage.

■ ADVICE FROM PROFESSIONALS: "Earned Media: Guidelines and Proven Techniques for First-Time Managers and Candidates," by Bob Wickers

You're about to manage your first campaign—a relatively small to mid-size race, possibly for county supervisor or city council. It's going to be competitive, and you're fortunate to have the kind of budget to afford a general consultant to handle message, overall strategy, and the paid media effort. But the budget is not quite big enough to afford a press secretary—that job falls to you.

In addition to coordinating day-to-day operations you're now also responsible for generating "earned" or "free" media—favorable press coverage that augments the campaign's overall message, bolsters the "paid" media, positions your opponent(s), and advances the goal of moving votes into your boss's column.

By following the few steps outlined below, your first foray into the world of shaping how the press covers a candidate and a campaign should be a successful one.

Media List & Relationships

First, assemble a comprehensive media list, which includes the name and contact information of every reporter who will cover your campaign —for every type of media outlet. For smaller races (particularly in rural and suburban areas) these outlets likely include one or two weekly newspapers, one or two local radio stations, and possibly one independent television station. In this environment, competition for news is relatively light, making it easier to obtain coverage for your candidate. If the campaign is set in an urban area within a large media market, your list will include several broadcast television stations and at least one major daily newspaper—making your job that much tougher in a highly competitive news market.

With your media list in hand, it's important to establish relationships right away. Visit with each reporter, political editor, and publisher of the weekly papers—as well as the reporters and news directors of local radio and television stations. These initial meetings should be informal and "off-the-record." The goal is to introduce yourself, so limit your discussion to a broad overview of the candidates and issues.

If you're hesitant about talking with the press, take heart in two important facts:

- **Many reporters working for small weekly papers and radio stations are rookies as well—young, generally inexperienced journalists covering politics for the first time.**

- They will be looking to you to provide them with news and compelling angles that will help them write the kind of stories that will earn them praise from their editors/publishers.

This is a mutually beneficial relationship you will be establishing. Members of the press have a job to do, and so do you. You need to remain in constant touch with these newly acquired contacts. Never be afraid to praise them for good work, and point out errors in their coverage when necessary—from day one to election night.

Write an Earned Media Plan

The most important parts of any political campaign are the beginning and the end. How a campaign is initially organized—how research data is integrated into message development, how target voter groups are identified, how budgets are created, etc.—is absolutely critical to its success. Just as a talented general consultant begins each race with a written campaign plan, a good press secretary begins with a comprehensive earned media plan of his or her own.

A winning earned media plan must consider:

- The overall message of the campaign. What is the theme? What are the issues this campaign will be decided on?

- Key voter groups. Who are the targets? What voter groups need to be moved in order to win?

- The general pace and timing of the campaign. Does the campaign have message "stages"? For example, does the campaign need to (1) introduce the candidate and bolster his or her image first, then (2) set up contrasts and draw issue comparisons with the opponent(s), and finally (3) attack? Is this the kind of race where the campaign can remain positive and simply work to attract favorable coverage throughout the race—coverage that augments the overall positive themes found in the campaign's "paid" media? Or, is this a challenge race that requires issue contrasts and attacks on an incumbent's record from day one?

Write your plan, and follow it.

Discipline, Creativity, News

Effective earned media efforts possess three basic, but essential, elements: message discipline, creativity, and the ability to make news.

For a press secretary, message discipline requires a deep understanding of what moves target voter groups; an ability to work closely, and in concert, with the general consultant and others involved in the paid media effort; a talent for keeping the candidate focused; and being able to recognize and correct message "drift."

Creativity is essential. Your candidate is the greatest asset to elicit positive coverage. Use him or her. At all times develop press availabilities, photo opportunities, sit-down visits with key reporters, editors, and publishers. Present or "sell" angles and story packages that are unique and further your message. For television, remember that backdrops matter. Where your candidate is standing is as important as what he or she is saying. Use the Internet and your campaign's Web site effectively—it's a tremendous tool to communicate to voters, campaign supporters, opinion leaders, donors, and members of the press.

Make news. Have something to say. Papering reporters with daily press releases is ineffective. Acquire and practice good judgment in the timing of releases, press conferences, and candidate availabilities. Staying in constant touch with reporters should provide you with a keen sense of when to move on a story and when to hold off.

Be advised: much of what you put out early in a campaign will not end up on the front page—or even the back page. Don't get frustrated by the lack of initial coverage. This is a campaign to be waged "over time." Much of your early work will be viewed as "background"—the process of educating individual reporters on issues, contrasts, and candidate attributes. Executed effectively, this early work will pay off to great benefit at the end of the campaign when reporters write candidate profiles and summaries, and when editorial endorsements are published.

Finally, every campaign is different; therefore no two earned media efforts are alike. The size and budget of a race, the number of media markets within the district, the presence of a competitive press, and the willingness of a candidate to aggressively court the media are just a few of the elements that will dictate the scope and direction of an earned media campaign. There is no "one-size-fits-all" approach; but there does exist a few general concepts, rooted in common sense, that are worth mentioning here: Do your homework. Be prepared. Anticipate the press's need for additional information, source citations, and contacts. Do your best to anticipate your opponent's earned media effort and attacks as well. Don't hide your candidate. Never say "no comment." Return your phone calls and be available at all times. Admit your mistakes immediately and never be afraid to apologize. . . . Rules to live by.

One last thing: don't call it "free" media. You earn it!

Bob Wickers is a national Republican campaign strategist and media consultant, whose clients include members of the U.S. Senate, governors, and major trade organizations. His firm is headquartered in San Francisco.

Developing a Press Kit

In order to make it easy for the press to contact you and to make yourself better known to key local reporters, send a press kit to all local media outlets at the beginning of your campaign. It should include the names and contact information of your staff, an indication that you will be available for comment, a list of local political issues that you are qualified to speak about, information on the campaign office and Web site, your campaign logo, pictures of you, your biography, your campaign literature, and any previous press coverage that you have received.

All of this information should be made available on the campaign Web site in a section for the media and should be available by request at the campaign office. Send a press kit to the news director at all local media outlets and any specific reporters you are targeting for coverage. Ask your staff to make follow up phone calls to these reporters and offer to set up an interview with you.

Sending Press Releases

Designate someone on the campaign staff who will regularly send updates to members of the media about major events in your campaign. If your press releases resemble newsletters, it is unlikely they will make it directly into print. Instead, provide information for a news story that you hope will be written. This means writing a strong headline and lead paragraph that will grab the reader's attention. You should emphasize the candidate's strengths, of course, but make your story about the candidate relevant to a local event or news item.

Press releases should be designed to make the reporter's job easier. A press release should include prewritten quotes from multiple sources, all of the critical information necessary to write a story (answer these questions: who, what, when, where, and why?), a statement about the relevance to readers of the information provided and its likely impact, and contact information for the candidate and campaign staff.

You do not have to send the same releases everywhere. If you become familiar with the stories covered by specific reporters at major news outlets, you may learn that they like a particular kind of story. If so, send them a release that fits with their preferred type of story or pitch them the story over the phone.

If you want reporters to attend an event, send them an invitation a week in advance in addition to a day-of-event press release. If you think a story has a chance to make it on the local news, your press release should emphasize the visuals of the event. After an event, you can make your own pictures and video available to local television as well.

■ **TAKE NOTE:**

A press release should be designed to make the reporter's job easier. It should include a strong headline and lead paragraph that grabs the reader's attention.

■ **LEARN MORE ON THE WEB:**

Find sample press releases that you can download and modify at campaigns.berkeley.edu.

Generating Letters to the Editor and Talk Radio Phone Calls

Not all media coverage of the candidate will come directly from your campaign. Encourage supporters to write letters to the editor and make phone calls to local radio stations. Organize a writing event or provide sample letters to the editor, although they will usually not be printed unless they seem personal. Make a list of local call-in radio programs available to your supporters and encourage them to call in with information about your campaign.

Interviews with the News Media

Once you have lined up interviews with journalists, be sure to make the most of them. Do not enter an interview without having prepared for it in advance. You should know something about the person who is interviewing you, especially what kind of stories he or she likes to write. Learn about the media outlet that the reporter works for and its likely audience. Preferably, you should know something about the story that the journalist is working on and its deadline. As you prepare for the interview, decide what your central message will be and how you will respond to obvious questions.

At your interviews, use short statements with simple language that gets to the point quickly. Come up with memorable quotations and important facts to incorporate into your answers. Use elements of your biography to emphasize your points. Use every opportunity to deliver your message but remember that reporters are unlikely to interview you again if you do not give them information that is relevant to the story they are writing. Whatever you do, do not lie or stretch the truth with reporters. If they find out, it will be detrimental to your campaign. Avoid saying anything that you do not want to be printed or broadcast, even if you are talking off the record.

In an interview, you should sound upbeat and positive. Do not get defensive if you are challenged. Admit any problems and describe how you are addressing them. If you are on television, make the most of the visual format by emphasizing your points with gestures and movement. Feel free to make the interview a conversation; ask the reporter questions and expand on points you made earlier.

If an interview is not going as well as you had planned, do not be resentful, continue to be polite. Remember that you will likely be interviewed again. Try not to get frustrated if you don't receive the access to the media that you want or if the interviews you give do not result in news coverage. It is very difficult to land interviews on television unless you are the hot news story of the moment; use other media when you are given the chance.

■ ADVICE FROM THE FRONT LINES: "Tips for Candidates: Generating Fair and Favorable Media Coverage," by Valerie Hyman

Facing the media is intimidating and it's difficult. This is true even under the best of circumstances because you know you have little or no control over what journalists do with your words and image. Still, there are a number of actions you can take to increase the chances coverage of you will be fair and perhaps even favorable.

To begin with, understand that citizens appreciate politicians who are confident and articulate, even when they disagree with their positions. They know clear thinking when they hear it. They smell deception and obfuscation a mile away.

You are most convincing when you speak off the cuff, rather than reading or reciting. You can do that when you have done your homework. The more prepared you are, the more confidence you exude. Knowing your material enables you to relax and speak fluently.

That said, it is fine to carry a few note cards with talking points on a variety of issues. Just be sure to use them as a quick reference rather than a crutch. Here are some other tips to use in facing the media:

1. Have your own agenda for every media encounter, from radio talk shows to neighborhood newsletters. Do you want to discuss mandatory testing for third graders? Or dredging the lake? Make sure you get your basic message across early in the encounter; you can expand on it later.

2. Get to your point quickly; do not beat around the bush. Say what you know and then stop. Sometimes the correct answer to a question is "I don't know." When appropriate, say you'll do some research and provide an answer later; then keep your promise.

3. Rehearse out loud. Speak to family or friends and encourage their honest feedback. Have someone videotape you as you articulate your ideas. Critique yourself: How interesting is the video? What questions have I left unanswered?

4. Find a focus for every news release, speech, major position, and
    weekly theme. Then reduce that focus to just three words—actor,
    action, subject of the action—in that order. For the third grade
    testing, for example: "Measurement improves teaching." Having
    a sharp focus clarifies your message and makes it easier for voters
    to understand. Articulating a laser sharp focus in three words takes
    lots of practice. Once you and your staff get the hang of it, you'll be
    thrilled with the results.

5. When you or someone on your staff make a mistake, take
    responsibility for it immediately and publicly as soon as you
    become aware of the problem. Apologize if appropriate. Nothing
    defuses anger like "I'm sorry." This goes for scandals as well as
    misstatements of fact.

6. Be prepared with clear and convincing evidence to substantiate
    your positions: history, precedent, photos, statistics, and survey
    information. Nothing persuades like "Just the facts, Ma'am."

7. Be conscious of your verbal and nonverbal habits. Learn to avoid the
    sounds, "Um" and "Uh," especially when beginning responses. Sit
    or stand still; avoid swaying and rocking whether you're on camera
    or on the phone. Consider hiring a coach; local theatrical directors
    and faculty at university speech therapy departments will be thrilled
    to work with you and charge reasonable rates for their services.
    Controlled, purposeful body language and speech communicate
    credibility and authority.

8. Be accessible. Make sure journalists can reach you 24 hours a day,
    seven days a week. Consider having a cell phone number just for
    journalists and keep that phone on and within earshot. The faster it
    is to get in touch with you, the sooner you prevent molehills from
    becoming mountains. Being easy to reach leads journalists to feel
    more comfortable with you, more willing to listen longer, and,
    surprisingly, less likely to call.

9. Journalists usually try hard to get their facts straight and to
    understand the issues they cover. Sometimes they are overworked

and underpaid. So when one of them does an especially good job of explaining a complicated issue or representing you fairly, give them a call or zap them an email to let them know you appreciate their effort.

Finally, keep in mind that the media are part of the bedrock of American democracy. The press is the only profession protected in the Constitution. That's because our founders knew this experiment in participatory democracy would not endure without the kind of dispassionate examination a free press can provide.

> ■ **BEST PRACTICE:** Make yourself as accessible as possible to the news media.

The job of the media is to give voice to the voiceless and hold the powerful accountable. Practice and preparation will ensure you are the first to hold yourself accountable to the people you serve.

Valerie Hyman has thirty years of experience working as a television reporter, newsroom manager, and corporate news executive. She is now president of The Management Coach and provides coaching and consultation for networks, station groups and their news directors.

Be a Guest on Talk Radio

Talk radio gives you the opportunity to fully present your positions and interact directly with voters. You can also plug events and generate volunteers for your effort. Making regular appearances on news, commentary, and call-in programs should be a priority.

Scheduling an appearance on these programs typically takes multiple phone calls and is never a guarantee. Identify every (relevant) radio program in your area and get to know the people at the stations. Keep records of the people you have contacted and your scheduled appearances. Have background materials ready to deliver to the station for their early use in promoting the program. Finally, let your supporters know when you will be on the radio and ask people to call in with supportive questions and comments.

Making Debates Central to the Campaign

When asked to name things that they like in campaigns, many voters have trouble but debates are usually mentioned. When asked what would improve campaigns, many voters say they would like to see more debates. Debates provide candidates with opportunities to speak directly to voters, and they serve as news events that generate free media for campaigns.

Scheduling debates and appearing at joint forums with your opponent(s) should be a priority of your campaign. If you get invitations to appear in debates, try to put them on the schedule early. Simply responding to requests, however, is not enough. You should offer to debate your fellow candidate(s) at different locations within the jurisdiction as part of your regular campaign schedule. Let the press know of your offer and ask them to sponsor one or more debates. Community organizations are another option for sponsoring debates; sponsored debates will result in higher attendance and news coverage.

If your opponent(s) will not participate in debates, you should make that an issue in the campaign. Tell voters why you think that the candidate does not want to debate and emphasize that debates are necessary to draw out relevant differences between the candidates. Ask organizations and the press to continue to request that the other candidates participate in debates. This will help bring attention to the openness of your campaign.

If you do schedule debates, research who the likely attendees will be and the level of news coverage the debates are likely to receive, as well as the format and topics that will be addressed. Prepare for the debates by having mock debates where your supporters stand in as your opponents and others ask you questions that you do not know in advance.

Participating in Town Hall Meetings and Community Events

Debates are not the only means by which candidates can interact with voters. Local organizations frequently sponsor question-and-answer sessions with candidates or invite candidates to address their members. Try to attend as many of these events as possible. If you are invited to speak to a group, make sure you set aside time before or after the event to meet voters and respond to their questions one-on-one.

Set up your own town hall meetings during the campaign. Many public venues, including schools and libraries, will make space available for your events. If you schedule a series of open meetings and heavily promote them on your campaign materials and at each of your events, you will be able to connect with many voters in person by the end of the campaign.

Many of the events will be sparsely attended, but this should not deter you from attending. If you establish yourself as an accessible candidate who is interested in meeting the voters—even in small numbers

■ WHAT DO VOTERS WANT?: More Candidate Debates

In our survey, we asked voters to list the "top two ways that you prefer to hear candidates communicate their messages to you—through speeches, debates, mailers, radio or TV call in shows, door-to-door, town hall meetings, or some other way?" Respondents expressed a strong preference for debates over any other mode of communication. Thirty-eight percent gave debates as their first choice and twenty-six percent mentioned debates as their second choice. Debates were the most popular second choice if respondents picked something other than debates as their first choice.

Focus group participants were equally supportive of debates. Some qualified their support for debates by making a distinction between "canned" or "orchestrated" debates and "real" or "meaningful" debates. Participants asserted that scripted debates, where the candidates are given the questions in advance, are mostly stagecraft, while unscripted debates and town hall meetings hold both substantive and symbolic value. Indeed, the focus group discussions suggested that debates serve different purposes for different voters:

- Debates provide cues to help voters with decision making. For Jeff, debates allow viewers to see how candidates respond under pressure, without a script, "That's how you can best get a handle on someone . . . there are no Tele-prompters, you know, it's on the spot. All of a sudden, they're hit with something and [we get to] see how they react to it."

- Debates are a means to learn about and assess a candidate's issue positions.

- Debates give voters a way to assess a candidate's truthfulness.

- A candidate's decision to participate (or not) in a debate holds symbolic value. Donald explains, "If there were three candidates and only two would debate that would make a big difference in my life. I would say, 'Why wouldn't they [debate]?' I'd be suspicious of it."

—voters will be more likely to believe that you will be an accessible officeholder. You will learn from these experiences and be able to incorporate feedback from voters into the campaign.

Create events that coincide with your campaign's door-to-door canvassing and phone banking. If you are targeting particular neighborhoods, identify facilities or houses in these neighborhoods where you can hold "meet and greets"—small gatherings where neighbors gather to meet you. Holding these types of events helps demonstrate to voters that you share their concerns. If you organize neighborhood events before your volunteers go door-to-door distributing your literature or make targeted phone calls, you can promote the events more easily.

> ■ **BEST PRACTICE: Promote debates.**
>
> Do more than participate when asked. Make scheduling debates a priority of your campaign.

Paid Media Strategies

Getting your message out often comes at a cost. Because reporters are not likely to give you the coverage you need and because it is difficult to talk to every voter before an election, your campaign will require some paid media to get your message out to voters.

The cost of paid media ranges from very little (constructing a simple Web site) to tens of thousands of dollars (television advertising). Your campaign budget and the size and scope of your race will dictate how much you can spend. No matter what your resources, develop a media strategy that is diverse enough to reach voters who prefer different news and entertainment outlets.

Developing a Web Site

A candidate Web site is an inexpensive way to give voters more of what they want: information about candidates—their backgrounds, qualifications, issue positions, key supporters, and what they hope to do when in office.

Web sites are great ways to:

- Include a relatively large amount of information that allows voters to compare candidates and learn more about the issues that they care most about.
- Keep in regular communication with supporters about the progress of the campaign.
- Provide voters with opportunities to interact with the campaign (which signals your willingness to listen).

Your Web site should look professional and, because the Web requires individuals to take action to visit your site, it must be attractive and well publicized. Produce at least a simple version of your site that can be up and running when you announce your candidacy and start distributing information about it. You can buy a domain name (such as joeformayor. com) for a small fee and typically pay about $20 per month for hosting. Some campaigns hire a professional Web developer but in most communities, you should be able to find a responsible student to develop and update the Web site for you for a nominal fee or even for free. Make sure that you secure a commitment to stay through the end of your campaign from whoever will act as your Webmaster. Once your site is up, put its address on all of your materials, including signs.

■ **BEST PRACTICE: Develop a campaign Web site.**

Provide voters with an easy way to learn more about your candidacy. Post your biography, issue positions, calendar of events, recent press releases, and a list of endorsements on your campaign Web site. Encourage voter participation by including ways for voters to interact with the campaign, such as a sign-up form for volunteer activities, an online donation form, and a way for voters to email you with comments or questions.

Make the Web site part of your broader communication strategy. Mention the Web site often as a source for more information about you and your campaign in speeches, advertisements, and conversations with voters. Encourage the press and volunteers to regularly check your Web site.

Use the site as a tool for your event planning, outreach to constituency groups, and volunteer organization. When you make claims about yourself or other candidates, make the Web site an extension of those claims by posting documentation for all to see. When you make policy speeches, encourage listeners who are interested in learning more to read the comprehensive position papers that you have posted on your Web site. Most will not read all of this information, but providing it establishes your reputation as an open and responsible potential officeholder.

At the very least, use your Web site to post information about your positions and your qualifications, press releases, a biography, a list of endorsements, a calendar of events, an email list sign-up form, a privacy policy for what you will do with personal information that the site collects, a form for donating money, and several options for how people can get involved in the campaign.

Better Web sites will include sections devoted to the central policy issues of the campaign, interactive tools voters can use to correspond with the candidate, extensive contrasts between the candidate and his or her opponent(s), a blog (web log) or diary, links to examples of the candidate's involvement with the community, and pages with the candidate's message to targeted constituencies.

The Web is an excellent medium for drawing contrasts because you can present visual aides (charts and tables) comparing your positions with those of other candidates and then link to documentation of those claims. You can even link to information from other candidates framed within your own commentary on their positions.

The Web is a valuable interactive medium because voters can send you information and select information they want to see. Keep track of pages voters visit to see what kinds of materials are of greatest interest to your visitors. Provide opportunities for feedback by incorporating a method to email the candidate and to provide feedback on the campaign or the Web site.

If you get many questions, you can post the questions and answers and allow people to browse through them. Many Web companies allow you to add bulletin boards and chat rooms to your site at no extra cost if you agree to show their advertisements. These interactive elements are fun for visitors but require more work from you or your staff to moderate the discussions.

Ideally, a Web site will deliver the candidate's message to undecided voters, but most visitors to the site will already be supporters. Communicating with these supporters and the press is another critical role for the Web site. Include news and site updates for people who visit regularly.

Update visitors on the latest from the campaign trail, including the activities of the candidate. A regularly updated blog by the candidate can keep visitors interested. You can include comments by supporters,

the volunteer coordinator, or the campaign manager in the blog. Make
sure that your directory of campaign staff and event calendar are updated
regularly and include information reporters or supporters might need to
contact the right person or find an event.

Prominently display several options for becoming more involved in
the campaign. Your financial contribution form should be easily found
from a link on the front page. Within one click, supporters should be able
to access information on the latest volunteer opportunities and events.
Use the Web site to build your organization. Post a request for precinct
captains and liaisons for particular organizations or communities and
have kits ready to send to those who seem most interested in building an
organization of volunteers in their neighborhoods.

Using Email Lists

Display an email sign-up form on your Web site for people who want
to be updated about the campaign. Collect email addresses of supporters
at your events and from those who call the office offering to help. You
should always ask permission to send them information using email.
Keep a complete list and a subdivided list for those who want different
kinds of information and internal communication.

Allow members to sign up for your list or unsubscribe easily. Subscription information, including instructions for how to unsubscribe,
should be included at the bottom of each message that you send. Always
ask supporters to forward your messages and ask their friends to sign up
for the list.

Use your email list to send information about upcoming events,
major endorsements, news coverage and appearances, volunteer activities, and responses to your opponent(s). If you can create humorous
ways to get your message across, you can use the power of forwarding
to get your message out to all of your supporters' friends. Keep everyone
updated regularly, but remember that every email you send may make
people less likely to pay attention to your next email.

Signs, Door Hangers, and Other Campaign Materials

Distributing and posting printed materials are a major part of local
political campaigning. These signs and materials improve your name
recognition, generate buzz about your candidacy in local conversations,

establish your momentum, and make voters more likely to pay attention to your other advertising efforts.

Use the same logo on all your materials and make your materials distinct from those of other candidates. Use simple and visible color schemes and stay away from colors of sports rivalries. For your signs, use simple text including your name and the office you are running for. Include your slogan and Web address if they are central to the campaign but do not clutter your signs with text. It is best not to

■ **BRIGHT IDEA: Question and Answer**

Keep in touch with your supporters using email and by adding an interactive component to your Web site that allows questions and answers or chats with the candidate.

change your logo, colors, or slogans midstream, so pretest your materials with voters and make sure that you are satisfied with them at the start of your campaign.

Shop around for low-cost printers or try to find a supporter who can donate in-kind printing. Keep track of your inventory and order as you go rather than buy everything you think you will need in advance. When you get the materials, keep them tidy so that you can easily find the materials you need.

Plan your sign strategy geographically. You should have at least two sizes of signs—large signs for major intersections and roads and small signs for the yards of your supporters. Use a large road map of your district or the jurisdiction where you are running when planning where to place your signs. You can often get average daily traffic counts from the county department of transportation.

Use the information in your database of voters to find the neighborhoods where support for you is most critical. Look up owners of the properties you are most interested in and ask them to post your signs. Identify the spots where other candidates have placed signs or ask candidates who have run for your office in the past for their lists of sign locations.

Check with the local regulatory authorities for any sign regulations and be sure to follow them. Never put signs in the public rights of way or in environmentally sensitive areas. Do not nail signs to trees and do not take other candidates' signs down. These activities will get you in trouble without bringing any benefit to your campaign.

Extensive yard signage allows supporters to feel involved and encourages neighbors to take a look at your campaign. You can print new and slightly different signs near the end of your campaign to signal to supporters that Election Day is coming. Some professionals recommend selling personalized signs to your supporters so that neighbors realize the personal nature of the campaign.

Door-hangers and leaflets can be a valuable part of your message delivery system. These materials should contain information about your qualifications, reasons for running, plans for the future, and/or key issue positions, but they should be easy to read so that you get your message across to voters who take only a few seconds to glance at them.

Direct Mail

Direct mail is one of the most common forms of mass advertising in campaigns. It presents a cost-effective way to reach your voters, especially when compared to television and radio advertisements. Unlike other forms of paid media, mailings can be sent to specific target audiences with messages tailored to their concerns.

A direct mailing, however, is only as effective as the mailing list used to deliver it. You should research your intended audience and study your voter rolls to make sure that you are sending information about your candidacy to the people you need to support you. For more targeted mailings, you can use organization lists or subscription lists.

Once the mailing reaches a member of your target audience, the next challenge is getting the recipient to read what you have sent. Research and carefully develop the content of your mailings. Find a way to make the mailing not look like junk mail. Consultants estimate that readers take only a few seconds (the time it takes to walk from the mailbox to the garbage can!) to read campaign mail. Assume that people will scan your mailings and make it possible for them to still get the message. Headlines need to draw the reader into the text; action photos that do not look posed can generate interest and support the written message.

Keep your message simple with graphics and emotionally stirring rhetoric but also document your claims with factual information. Broad claims with no supporting evidence or third-party support are not typically believed. Use humor and references to popular culture or current events to get people interested in what you have to say. Pretest each mailing and make sure that you look at a final proof before it goes to press.

It is less expensive to label and process your own mail than to hire an outside firm, but it's also important to avoid potential headaches. Making an error with regard to the format of the piece or following postal regulations (for example, by not including the bulk mail permit for the right post office) can result in a mailing that will not get sent. The mailing needs to be "red tagged" (to indicate that it is a political mailing that can be sent first class at a third-class rate) and correctly sorted (that is, organized by zip code). For assistance, contact the business center at your central post office.

■ ADVICE FROM PROFESSIONALS: "Developing a Campaign Mail Piece," by Mitchell Englander

From mailbox to trashcan, you have only two seconds to grab a voter's attention. Remember, if it's hard to read, they won't! Direct mail is one of the most important tools that campaigns can use to reach voters effectively and affordably. It is worth taking the time to develop campaign mail that will be read and remembered.

There is more to producing effective direct mail than meets the eye. There are many parts that have to come together seamlessly; assembling all of them is crucial for creating effective direct mail. Here are five basic steps to follow when developing your mail:

1. Your list is your life.

One of the most important elements of the mail campaign is a clean and up-to-date voter file. Whatever you do, don't cut costs or corners on your voter file. Remember, garbage in equals garbage out.

The voter file must use the most comprehensive and current data available and should be householded with enhanced information that includes at least the twelve basic information fields:

1. Name
2. Mailing Information (with Carrier Route and Zip+4)
3. Districts (including current precinct numbers)
4. Telephone Numbers

5. Party Affiliation
6. Gender
7. Date of Birth
8. Voter History
9. Voter Registration Date
10. Ethnicity (appended via surname dictionaries)
11. Homeowner or Renter
12. Email Address (or at least a field to append one during the campaign)

Have an experienced campaign computer technician manage your voter files. Although there are many political database companies that offer voter files in a variety of formats and campaign software to manage your mailing lists, you don't want to accidentally send your Jewish Democrat/Soccer Mom "Happy Mother's Day" mailer to 75-year-old Republican Asian men!

2. Plan early and plan ahead.

Once you have your voter file in place, you can start to develop your mail plan. Map out each piece—format and content, targeted universe, budget, and a conservative production timeline. Invariably there will be a hold-up somewhere: a difficult approval process, printing and lettershop problems, a mail house company behind schedule, or a post office that sits on your mail. Build in several extra days to a week to account for the unknown.

3. Choose a format.

There are nine categories of political direct mail that will best communicate your message.

1. Introduction-puff/Biography
2. Issue driven
3. Accomplishments
4. Attack (aka: negative or hit piece)
5. Comparison
6. Third-Party Testimonials (endorsements, groups, organizations)
7. Geography (based on issues affecting the area where you live)

8. Thematic
9. Values/Ideology

Every message in the campaign can be communicated using one of these formats. Each format has a very clear and unique objective. Sometimes you can get away with mixing some of the formats in one piece, just don't make a rule of it. As an example, an attack piece may be negative against the opposition on the front and inside, with a positive third party testimonial about your candidate on the back.

4. Develop your message.

Once you have your voter file, a plan in place, and a format in mind, it's time to develop your message. Designing for political targeted direct mail is a pragmatic endeavor. Concept, copy, and photos should be compelling. Use photos, incorporate themes, and include copy that conveys your overall campaign message.

The text is important, but the critical parts for the voters are the visuals. Use powerful graphics and pictures, including a color scheme that stands out but is easy on the eye. Leave lots of "white space" (the space around your text and visuals that is left blank)—it makes the piece easy to read. Also, don't forget that most high propensity voters are seniors and small type is hard to read for them.

5. Use effective design.

You must catch the voter's eye and intrigue him enough to stop and read a little. If the copy isn't any good then great design can't salvage it. Assuming you have good copy, develop a design that grabs the reader by the throat and doesn't let go until you've gotten your message across.

Shy away from using the "good old fashioned" political colors and logos. If you do, your mail will simply blend in with all the other political mail that the voter receives.

After the headline, the most read part of the letter is the "P.S."—if you're sending out a letter-type mailing, always put your number-one message in the P.S. People also read the captions on photos—always put informative captions on the photos you use. If a paragraph is particularly important, make it extremely short (2-3 lines) or use a "drop-cap" capital letter to start the paragraph—either one will make it more likely to be read by people who are just "skimming" your piece. Remember, almost everyone scans first, to see if reading the piece is worth his time. That's why you must always design for both "scanners" and "studiers."

There are two types of "scanners." One "scanner" may simply look at the front on the way to the trashcan, and the other may open your piece and briefly read through it. Prepare for both scenarios.

Make sure that the cover of the mailer includes the candidate's name in large type, a picture of the candidate, and the campaign slogan—that's it. This way, if a voter simply looks at your piece before throwing it away (or recycling it, to be politically correct), he will still see the candidate's name, picture, and message. For those who scan the inside before discarding your literature, include big, bold headlines, picture captions, and emphasis—such as underlines, bolding, and highlighted words where appropriate. Do not use excessive emphasis like mixing highlighting, underlining, and bold in the same piece—it gets too busy and then no one will read it.

Some voters, however, will study your piece in-depth. Include plenty of information for these "studiers" by providing additional information below your headlines and throughout your bio and issues paragraphs.

Some other rules for layout and design:

- *Use quality photos!* There is no substitution for professional photography. Even the best designs turn sour with shoddy photography. Dark eyes or a hint of a five-o'clock shadow because of bad lighting overpower the reader with negative thoughts about the candidate or issue. If you must use digital photography, turn up the pixels! If you like grainy and pixilated photos, start writing your concession speech!

- *Think clean—be clean.* Graphics are meant to enhance your message and draw the voter to read or respond. Too many graphic images and font types portray a cluttered mind and will garble your message. The graphic on the cover of your mailer will be the main factor in increasing its chances of being read. Since the postal worker places the mail label-side up in the box, be sure to include graphic images and a strong headline on the side to be labeled. First impressions are lasting. They set the tone for your message and must intrigue the recipient to read on.

- ***Use color.*** Proper use of color adds to the perceived credibility and quality of the candidate and adds realism to the issues and message. Whenever possible, use full color. Many novices avoid using color because they fear being viewed as "slick." Never equate color with "slickness." Color works! In every medium the public sees color—color TVs, color billboards, color newspapers. Even *The New York Times* uses color. Color lets the public see your candidate in the flesh and allows them to see him as a real person. Avoid using a barrage of conflicting bright colors. Black and red are usually reserved for negative pieces. Also, stay away from simply red, white, and blue.

- ***Punch your words.*** Keep your message brief and to the point. Write copy that gets read, not copy that puts voters to bed. Use big headlines and jumbo quotes, with supporting text never smaller than 12-point type. Place text adjacent to photos or graphic images wherever possible. Clever use of folds and text blocking helps break up the clutter if the message is complicated.

- ***Do the "flash test."*** Many people read their mail while standing over the kitchen wastebasket. The "flash test" ensures that your mailer, if tossed after the briefest of glances, will leave some impression with the reader. This is your safety catchall test for every mail piece you send. Take your mock up and hold it up to a noncampaign participant for two seconds per side. Then ask . . . did they get the message? What is the candidate's name?

- ***Don't forget to proof!*** Finally, before signing the "approved to print with no changes" form . . . proof, proof, proof—but don't try this at home alone. Give it to someone who you know and trust outside the campaign to proof for spelling, grammar, content, and readability.

Now you're ready to go to print!

Mitchell Englander is a political strategist and founder of Issue Strategies, Inc., a southern California government relations and political consulting firm specializing in targeted message development and tactical implementation.

Radio and Television Advertisements

If you want to communicate with a mass audience and you have the funds, you should consider using radio and television advertising. Each has different strengths that require different strategies and scripts. Radio ads are more effective than television ads for targeting audiences based on demographics. Television ads can provide a more powerful and memorable visual message.

When developing radio ads, pay attention to the script; take the time to get the wording right. It does not have to look right on the page as long as it sounds good, for example, you do not need to use complete sentences. Do not overuse sound effects or professional announcers. You want real people who do not sound canned rather than furniture salesman and jingles.

You can use radio to draw the listener in with questions or talk directly to your opponent(s) in the ad. Your message should be simple and not excessively political; if you make an ad that sounds political right away, you are likely to lose part of your audience. Radio works better if the message addresses a topic that is a part of regular conversation at the time.

Radio advertisements can be expensive, so placement is critical. Placing ads during drive time gets you the largest audience but you can get cheaper rates by running your ads at less popular times. If you advertise during news and talk programs, you may get more attentive listeners but they are also more likely to have made up their minds. Find out about the audience that each station serves and make sure it matches your target voters. For music stations, comic or light-hearted ads might be more effective.

Producing and buying airtime for television advertisements is a complex process that normally requires professional help. If you decide to do it yourself, you will need to set up a shoot with video or film, have the ad edited, and then buy time slots for airing the ad on network and cable television stations.

Creating a political ad requires extensive preproduction planning, a major production phase, and follow-up. You will need to take into account production values like script and lighting, timing, transitions between images, and locations in addition to concept and message. If the candidate looks bad or the advertisement looks low quality, it can have a negative effect on the viewers' opinions of the candidate.

Here are two cheaper formats for television ads that can be effective:

- The candidate talks directly into the camera about why he or she is running for office or responds to an opponent's attack by laying out the facts of a matter and, if appropriate, apologizing for any improprieties.
- Several residents give unscripted testimonials about the candidate's achievements and fitness for office.

Most candidates advertise on network television, especially during the local news, in an attempt to reach a large number of voters. This can be prohibitively expensive, however, and your ads can get caught in the clutter. You can use cable television for cheaper spots and better targeting. The cable company can run ads on specific channels at specific times. Stations with viewers who are likely voters include 24-hour news networks, weather and travel channels, business channels, and movie classics channels. You can also target your spots at men and women, using networks aimed at those audiences. Wherever you run your ads, test them beforehand with focus groups or impromptu sessions with voters to make sure your message is getting across.

Newspaper and Print Advertising

Most campaigns do not use newspaper advertising because it is not an effective medium for conveying emotion and generating a response. Newspaper readers are likely voters, however, and could be an attractive target audience in some constituencies. Newspaper ads offer an effective way to compare candidates' positions using visual aides (charts, tables) or to supplement the coverage your campaign is receiving by presenting your positions in your own words. Newspaper ads are good for announcing endorsements and telling voters about special elections.

> ■ **BEST PRACTICE:** Document your claims, no matter what medium you use for advertising.

There are other print advertising options as well. Research the local market and what people read in your area. If a publication is read widely or read by an audience that you want to reach, consider placing an ad in it.

■ **WHAT DO VOTERS WANT?: Informative Advertising and Documentation of Negative Claims**

Survey respondents were asked whether they found television advertisements helpful for making voting decisions. Predictably, more than two-thirds (68%) said the ads were "not too helpful" or "not at all helpful." Focus group participants shared this perception of television ads as mostly unhelpful, even though they rejected the idea of longer (two minute) ads.

Asked how candidates might change their ads to make them more helpful, Anna replied, "On those rare occasions when they talk about what they're for, and they don't mention their opponent, I try to listen, which is when I feel like the candidate is turning to the camera and just being as honest as politicians can be." Colleen agreed, "Instead of ... quoting something about the other person, just have the candidate talk to you. 'This is what I believe in. This is what I want to do.'"

Other participants were more accepting of candidates including negative statements in their advertisements as long as they supported the claims they were making with facts. Documentation of negative claims can be essential to making an attack appear credible to voters. Donald explains, "If an attack brings out information, and can be validated, it can be useful, but if it is just a general statement, then you don't have the credibility."

Internet Advertising

Internet advertising can be used for highly specific targeting or cheaper message delivery, but it is difficult to reach all the voters in your constituency using this medium. You can often get good deals on banner advertising with local newspapers or publications and you can contract with large Internet Service Providers or Portals to deliver banner ads only to people who live in your district or local jurisdiction. You can expect higher click-through rates by placing general ads on news sites and targeted messages on special interest sites.

Use banner ads to broadcast a message and to drive people to your site. Ads can be effective at encouraging new visitors to come back to the site and sign up for email from the campaign. They can also be used to promote a particular online feature such as a tax calculator that allows voters to compare the benefits of a candidate's tax plan with her opponent's, or to announce a chat with the candidate. Most people (at least 99.5%) will not click on your ad, so make sure they can absorb the message within the banner.

Steer clear of sending unsolicited email. Recipients are quite sensitive about their email and candidates that have used "spam" are likely to generate many more complaints than new supporters. Sending unsolicited emails is likely to generate negative news stories and irate recipients who may call the office and jeopardize your computer security.

Developing a Media Plan

Rather than make decisions in an ad hoc fashion, develop a media plan at the beginning of your campaign. It should include the kinds of outlets you will use, the kinds of advertising you will engage in, the kinds of messages you will communicate to the voters, and how much you will spend. Even though advertising usually requires advance work, plan for contingencies and be prepared to adapt your plan to the concerns of the moment.

When evaluating how much paid media to purchase, consider the cost-effectiveness of various kinds of paid media in terms of the number of target voters reached, the cost of producing and placing the advertisement, and the likely impact of the ad. Consultants claim that voters must be exposed to a paid message ten times before they remember it. So purchase enough spots to ensure that the ad gets the voters' attention. Set aside some funds for the final weeks of the campaign, so you have the resources to counter any last-minute negative attacks that might be launched against you.

Whether you choose direct mail, radio ads, television ads, or another form of paid advertising to get your message out, make sure your advertising works together and that messages in different venues reinforce one another. Some professionals recommend that you develop themes for your paid and free media that reinforce your message of the month, the week, or the day.

Finally, if you combine multiple advertising methods with direct voter contact, you are likely to reach all of your target audience multiple times. Ideally, by the time your paid messages reach your audience, voters will already have developed positive views of you from hearing about you in other venues (for example, free media, direct voter contact), and thus will be more receptive to your message.

Conclusion: Five Things to Know about Delivering Your Message

1. Repeat, repeat, repeat.

Repeating your message is just as important as being clear, concise, and compelling. Remember that you are competing for people's scarce attention. At any given time, your communication is likely to reach different audiences. Typically it takes several exposures to a message for it to reach the recipient. Although it may seem tedious, consistently delivering your key campaign message will increase the likelihood that your target voters will hear it.

2. Earn free media.

Make yourself available to reporters and actively promote news stories and news events. Deal with the media professionally and make their job easier. Be prepared for interviews and make your appearances count.

3. Make debates and public events central to your campaign.

Make a commitment to participate in public forums and debates with your fellow candidate(s) and organize your own series of town-hall meetings to talk directly to voters. Use your willingness to debate and talk to voters to develop a reputation as an accessible candidate.

4. Complement your grassroots campaign work with an effective Web site and good campaign materials.

Even if you plan to run an on-the-ground campaign, you need to produce an effective Web site and email list to coordinate your organization. You need good campaign literature to distribute and quality signs in visible locations to demonstrate your widespread support.

5. Use a diverse and cost-effective advertising strategy.

There are many options for campaign advertising, some more expensive than others. You can use direct mail and the Web to target your key constituencies and, if you have the resources, radio and television to reach mass audiences with professional messages. Develop a media plan to make all your advertising work together to deliver your message effectively.

7

127

Advertising can only get you so far in local elections. You need to make direct contact with voters and mobilize them to turn out on Election Day. To do this, you will need to build a strong field operation and plan your strategies for contacting and mobilizing your voters. This is known as your "ground game."

At the beginning of your campaign, figure out how many votes you will need to win. Then spend the rest of the campaign building your list of supportive voters so that you can mobilize them on Election Day (and even before, if they vote absentee). Use door-to-door canvassing, phone calls, and other forms of direct contact to identify likely voters who support you, to persuade undecided voters to support you, and to mobilize both of these populations to vote for you. Your ability to achieve each of these objectives will determine the overall success of your campaign.

Calculating the Number of Votes You Need to Win

The calculus that determines the outcome of an election is quite simple—to win, a candidate needs to receive one more vote than his or her opponent(s). The hard part is figuring out the total number of votes that you will need to win and where they will come from. When calculating this number, consider the following questions:

- How many votes did the winner of the last (contested) election receive?
- How many registered voters are there in the district or jurisdiction?
- What percentage turned out the last time this office was contested?
- Is there anything else on the ballot that is likely to drive up turnout this time, or anything missing from the ballot that will decrease turnout?

Once you have determined the number of registered voters in your district or local jurisdiction and the likely turnout (based on past, comparable elections), you can estimate the total number of voters that you will need to vote for you. If you have only one opponent and only one candidate will be elected, you will need 50% plus one vote. If you have more than one opponent competing against you but only one candidate will be elected, you will only need a plurality of the vote. In either case, to ensure a sufficient margin of victory, you should set your vote target higher than the total number of votes you will need to win.

If you are running in an election where multiple candidates will be chosen, calculating the total number of votes you will need to win is more difficult. In addition to the questions above, you must assess the strength of the other candidates in the race. How many candidates will likely receive little or no support? How many will be competitive for winning the most votes? Is support among a particular constituency (such as conservatives) likely to be split between two main candidates? These questions are necessary because the number of votes needed to win will depend on how well the other candidates perform.

For example, if the three candidates who receive the most votes will be elected to fill three seats, you will not need to win a plurality of votes. You will only need to come in third to win. In these elections, however, voters typically cast multiple votes, making calculations of votes needed to win even more complicated. Your best strategy is to consider the specific circumstances of your race, such as the number of candidates, the rules of the election, and the character of your jurisdiction. Then set a realistic vote target that will allow you to win your election comfortably.

Identifying and Targeting Voters

Before you can contact and mobilize your voters, you need to know who they are. Start by obtaining a voter file from the county elections official that lists registered voters in your district or in the jurisdiction where you are running and whether they voted in past elections. Ask a volunteer to transfer this information to a database that is kept separate from the database of potential donors and the volunteer list. Larger campaigns may want to hire a professional to help compile the voter database. Either way, make sure your database remains private and secure.

Third-party vendors sometimes sell voter lists with demographic information (for example, age, marital status, ethnicity) that can be entered into your database and used to target mail, get-out-the-vote, and other campaign activities. At minimum, your database should identify the party affiliation and voting history of the registered voters in your district or jurisdiction.

After you obtain a list of registered voters and set up your voter database, the next step is to identify voters who support you, support your opponent(s), or are undecided. The object is to move those in the undecided column over to the column of voters who support you through free and paid media, persuasive mail, phone calls, door-to-door canvassing, and other forms of direct contact.

> ■ **BRIGHT IDEA: Develop a Voter Contact Tracking System**
>
> Every campaign needs a system to identify likely voters who support the candidate and then make sure those voters do indeed vote. Provide your door-to-door or phone canvassers with record keeping tools (e.g., note cards, call forms) so the campaign can enter the results of the canvass into the voter database.

Campaigns in relatively small districts or local jurisdictions with a large volunteer base can implement a voter identification program that involves calling all of the voters on the voting rolls to find out if they are committed to a candidate. This information is entered into the voter database. Supportive voters receive get-out-the-vote calls and materials near the end of the campaign and "convincible" voters (those who are undecided) are called again, visited by canvassers, and sent information through the mail. When making voter identification calls, your volunteers should be clear that they are calling from the campaign and attempting to talk to all voters. Otherwise, they may be accused of "push polling," which means disguising a persuasive phone call as an independent poll.

If your campaign does not have the resources needed to call all of the registered voters in your district or jurisdiction, you should develop a list of targeted voters based on the demographic and geographic information provided in the voter rolls. Choose the relevant characteristics that will allow you to narrow your list of potential supporters to a reasonable size. Then ask your volunteers to contact these likely voters using door-to-door canvassing or phone banking in order to determine their level of support.

Targeting Makes Best Use of Limited Resources

Most campaigns have limited resources, including candidate and volunteer time. Use these resources efficiently in ways that are most likely to advance your ultimate goal of winning the election. Some professionals recommend expending 80% of your campaign resources on undecided likely voters and using the remaining 20% to mobilize your base. This general rule needs to be tempered with your own political judgment, but it is a good starting place in planning how to allocate your campaign resources.

Targeting involves focusing your resources on specific groups of voters based on their party affiliation, likelihood of voting, geographic location, or other demographic characteristics such as ethnicity, gender, or religious affiliation. It requires that you adapt your message to the concerns of your audience. The mail you send to targeted voters, the scripts you use when you talk to these voters, and the literature you drop off in door-to-door canvassing should all be adapted to emphasize aspects of your message that will appeal to your targeted voters. If your voter database is set up correctly, you should be able to use it to help with your targeting efforts, including sending targeted direct mail, developing call lists for targeted phone banking, and compiling household lists for door-to-door canvassing.

Making Direct Contact with Voters

Many voters expect to know their local representatives and to connect with them on a personal level. To gain the voters' trust and support, you will need to talk directly to them. The more contact voters have with you, the more they will learn about you and know that you are in tune with their concerns.

Although television and radio advertisements can provide effective means for communicating your message, research has shown that speaking directly to voters is more likely than mass advertising to generate participation and support, especially in local elections. Direct contact with voters can also help you establish a reputation as a hard-working candidate who cares what voters have to say.

Most successful campaigns combine advertising and direct contact with voters to get their messages out. The most common forms of direct contact are telephone calls and door-to-door canvassing. Both require volunteers and a well-organized field operation.

Setting Up a Phone Bank

Setting up a phone bank of volunteers who call registered voters is an efficient way to reach a large number of voters in a short amount of time. Providing your volunteers with training before they begin calling is critical to the success of your phone bank. Your volunteers will be interrupting people at home, so make sure that they know how to make calls that are brief, effective, and help convince voters to support your candidacy rather than turn them off.

Your volunteers should begin the call by saying that they are not calling to sell anything and that they are volunteers for your campaign. Develop a script for your callers to ensure a consistent message, but it is important that your callers not simply read a script; they should be willing and able to respond to voters' questions and concerns. To instill confidence in your callers and ensure a smooth message delivery, make sure your callers practice on each other before they start dialing. Ask them to keep track of whom they reached (and didn't) and how the voters responded.

Phone banks can be an early-warning system to alert you to the concerns of voters. Many campaigns use phone banking to gather information as well as distribute it. Formal polling is typically done by phone, but it requires professional procedures that should not be attempted by volunteers. Phone banks can provide valuable informal feedback, however, and you should be attentive to the message from the grassroots. Keep tabs on the messages your opponent(s) deliver by phone and mail, as well. Your callers should always be prepared to respond to questions about the latest attacks launched by your opponents.

Political telemarketing is more accepted than commercial telemarketing, but many people are still annoyed by the interruptions. Remind your callers to be polite even when they are not received well. Automated calls are expensive and less effective, but they can be used to mobilize supporters in combination with other methods of direct contact.

Setting Up a Door-to-Door Canvassing Operation

Many local campaigns use door-to-door canvassing to demonstrate their grassroots support and to meet voters directly. Before setting up the canvass, take a driving tour of your district or jurisdiction and assess the feasibility of walking around it. Try to determine whether your constituents will react positively to getting a chance to meet you or your volunteers, and whether the other candidate(s) in the race will walk door-to-door, which might create the expectation among voters that you will do the same.

If your district or jurisdiction is large or you have a small number of volunteers and are unable to canvass all of it, start with your strong areas, move into the swing areas, and finish in the strong areas. It is a good idea to focus on homes with multiple voters and analyze past voting returns to identify densely populated swing precincts.

The success of your door-to-door canvassing operation will depend on the strength of your organization. If you have a base of supporters at the precinct level, you can set up a system of regional coordinators, precinct captains, and block captains. While voters prefer direct contact with the candidate, the second best option is volunteers who are neighbors of the voters they canvass.

Try to coordinate your canvass with your other campaign efforts. For example, send mail before you walk so that voters already know something about you before you or your volunteers reach their door. Distribute a different set of materials when you meet them. For those households where no one is home, leave a door hanger with a short, hand-written note on it and follow up by phone or mail.

Volunteers are more likely to participate if you can promise them a regular schedule of precinct walking that includes a short training and a thank-you party. Each time they walk, you should provide them with a good map and a list of houses to visit. Ask about their experiences when they return.

Going Door-to-Door

Before you start walking, you will need to estimate the time it will take you to complete your rounds and build a reasonable schedule. An average door-to-door contact requires three to five minutes. Remember that many residents will not be home, and weather conditions can affect the time it takes to get around. Keep these factors in mind when developing a schedule that you can actually complete.

Be polite and smart about your visits. If a voter does not agree with you on something, it is best to acknowledge your difference of opinion and move on rather than enter into an argument that will waste valuable time. Do not get discouraged by rude people or slammed doors; they are inevitable. Do not walk at night or at times of the day when no one is likely to be home. Dress well but not so that you look out of place in the neighborhood. As always, stretch before walking and drink plenty of water.

Use a nametag or campaign button to identify yourself. Introduce yourself and the office you are seeking, and explain your reasons for running in a brief (thirty seconds or less), clear statement. Turn your contact with voters into a conversation rather than a speech by soliciting questions and asking about their concerns. Keep track of whom you talk to, the number of registered voters in the household, the issues that they care about, and the level of their support, but do not take notes until after your conversation. If voters express support for you, ask them if they would agree to place a sign in their yard. If a voter seems especially enthusiastic, ask him to volunteer a few hours of time on the campaign. Take advantage of street life; talk to people who are outside but do not interrupt their activities.

■ **BRIGHT IDEA: Convert Your Endorsements into Resources for Your Campaign**

One of the benefits of winning endorsements from local groups is the potential cadre of supporters that they can offer your campaign. Be sure to recruit and use the volunteer base of these organizations for the direct contact activities of your campaign.

If volunteers are walking on your behalf, ask them to follow these guidelines. Impress upon them that they are representing you and the campaign and need to remain respectful and polite. Have them begin their contact with a voter by introducing themselves as volunteers for your campaign and saying why they are involved. Teach them how to assess the likely support of those they visit and how to adjust their scripts based on the voters' attitudes and concerns. If your volunteers are neighbors of people they canvass, ask them to invite their neighbors to a get-to-know-the-candidate event at their home. By planning local house parties for the days immediately following the canvass, you can turn the walk into a full-scale neighborhood mobilization.

Follow up

Always send follow-up letters or post cards after calling or canvassing. Lock up the commitment of voters who said they are planning to vote for you by sending them a letter or post card thanking them for their support. Send a different letter or card to undecided voters. Mention your call or visit, thank them for their time, include any information they may

■ WHAT DO VOTERS WANT? Candidates Who Make Direct Contact With Voters

As with unscripted debates, focus group participants praised the substantive and symbolic benefits of candidates who participate in town hall meetings, make personal appearances, and go door-to-door. These forms of interactive communication make it possible for voters to receive a direct response to their questions. They allow voters to size up a candidate ("look him in the eye") and gauge the candidate's sincerity. Victoria explains the benefits of candidates who canvass:

> You could ask anything you want, and they're there. The one that's running for city council of my district came over a few days ago. And she was there for a little bit, and she wasn't with anybody else, so she wasn't there with somebody telling her what she should be saying or anything. She was just giving out her flyer and telling us what she was for, what she was going to do. And we could ask anything. She even asked, 'Was there anything else you want to ask me?' So that's good.

Another focus group participant, Richard, makes a similar point:

> One of the local city council guys showed up at my door the other day. And I thought that was pretty impressive. . . . I opened the door and he just said who he was, he's running for city council. He wasn't there to give me a huge pitch, but I could tell that if I had asked him a few questions, he would have answered them. And so I think that's another nice way to do it. . . . It can only happen at a local level, but, you know, getting out there in person goes a long way.

Some participants interpret the effort involved in making direct contact with voters as concern for the voter and evidence that the candidate will work hard once in office. Jeff suggests the symbolic importance of candidates who go door-to-door, "I would say [candidates] would have to be enthusiastic about it to go through the footwork of it. [. . .] It tells us they're genuine, you know."

have requested, and explain again why you are the best person for the job. Voters who were not reached should receive a letter or card introducing you to the voter. It should mention that you attempted to contact them and ask them to consider supporting you in the upcoming election.

Communicating with Different Kinds of Audiences

As you meet with prospective voters, you will notice that not everyone shares the same concerns or views and not everyone prefers the same kind of political interaction. Before you speak to local groups or canvass

■ **BEST PRACTICE: Set aside time every week to make direct contact with voters.**

By doing so, you satisfy the voters' desire for direct contact with candidates, give them an opportunity to be heard, and hone your public speaking skills.

a neighborhood, learn about the issues affecting the community and the concerns of its members. It is important to adapt to local customs and establish trust among your listeners. One effective tactic is for you or a member of your campaign to attend one of the group's meetings before you are scheduled to speak to its members. This will help you find the right tone for your remarks.

■ **WHAT DO VOTERS WANT? Different Types of Information**

When our survey asked respondents what they want to learn most about the candidates—issues, experience, character, intelligence, party platform, campaign practices, or something else—most chose issues as their first choice (43%). However, there was notable variation among respondents concerning what they want to learn. While 57% of those with postgraduate study expressed their preference for learning about the candidate's stands on issues, only 23% of those without a high school degree chose issues as their first choice. Instead, 33% of respondents with some high school or less chose "experience" as their first choice, compared to only 8% of respondents with postgraduate study.

We also found differences with regard to respondents' interest in learning about the candidate's character. Character was a more popular choice among older respondents, among Republicans, and among conservatives. Thirty-five percent of conservatives cited character as their first choice, but only 18% of liberals did. The following exchange between focus group participants Charles and Penny, who identify as Republicans, and Jeff, a Democrat, exemplifies this liberal/conservative difference on the issue of character, underscoring the differences between voters and what they consider to be relevant information about the candidates:

CHARLES: Politicians can be role models, and I wouldn't want my children looking up to someone whose morality is different than what I'm trying to teach my children.

JEFF: I try not to think of their personal image as much. I just try to look at it as if it's a job to be filled. And on the job application, they don't ask, 'What is your sexual preference? What is your religious background?' None of that should come into it. It's how well you can do the job.

PENNY: But who you are is what you do. And this is America, and we do have a heritage to protect. And so character does play a part in how they handle their job, because they're making public decisions. And they sign the final papers.

In general, some voters will be informed about politics and interested in the specific details of your issue positions while others who are less involved in politics will be more interested in obtaining easy cues about your fitness for office and your general political orientation. As you campaign, be responsive to the different levels of interest among voters and adapt your message accordingly. If they do not seem interested, don't risk boring your audience with the details of your policy proposals; some voters will only want to be assured that you have the experience and dedication needed to be an effective officeholder. Always make time for voters to ask you questions and express their concerns. Be sensitive to differences in ethnic, religious, economic, and geographic communities in your jurisdiction and adapt your style of presentation accordingly.

■ WHAT DO VOTERS WANT? Different Forms of Campaign Communication

Not only are voters interested in different things about candidates, they prefer to be communicated with by campaigns in different ways. Although voters overwhelmingly prefer debates as the primary mode of campaign communication, our analysis revealed considerable variation among subgroups of survey respondents. Men are more likely to prefer debates than women (42% vs. 34%); so are the well educated—46% of those with postgraduate study prefer debates compared to 30% of those with some high school. Respondents with the least amount of education expressed a greater preference for call-in shows (29%, compared to only 9% of those with postgraduate study). Younger voters (18-24) are more likely to prefer speeches (20%) and call-in shows (22%) than are older respondents (11% and 16%, respectively).

When asked if television ads are helpful for making voting decisions, 42% of those with a high school degree said that ads are "somewhat" or "very helpful," compared to only 17% of those with postgraduate study. Older respondents were less likely to find ads helpful than younger respondents. Forty-eight percent of respondents between the ages of 18 and 24 said ads are "somewhat" or "very helpful" compared to only 24% of respondents who are fifty-five or older. Whites are the least enthusiastic about ads—only 24% find them helpful. By contrast, African Americans, native and naturalized Latinos, and naturalized Asians all have a more positive opinion of campaign ads (49%, 46%, 50%, and 48%, respectively, found ads to be "somewhat" or "very helpful").

These findings suggest that candidates who are interested in targeting specific audiences may want to select modes of communication that correspond to their audience's preferences.

Talking to Undecided Voters

Over the course of your campaign you will be speaking to lots of groups and individual voters. It is best to develop a short speech that you can use for any occasion and then make adjustments to it as you speak to different audiences. Do not overuse clichéd political language and be careful not to use technical language or appear to be aloof. You should be conversational but serious about your candidacy.

When you talk about issues, state the problems that motivated you to act before listing your achievements. Describe what you plan to do next rather than focusing on past mistakes. Do not give detailed accounts of how you developed your policy proposals; instead, talk about issues in terms of problems and solutions that affect the voters.

If you can, make the topic personal by including elements of your biography when describing the motivations behind your proposals. If you use comedy, tell short jokes that do not seem contrived and move quickly to the serious point that your jokes raise. As you speak to large audiences, select several people to make eye contact with at different places in the room and rotate among them.

In general, your interactions should leave voters with the impression that you want to establish an ongoing relationship with them. Encourage your listeners to participate in the conversation by asking them to ask questions and by soliciting their ideas. Make sure you listen as well as speak.

As with all skills, practice makes perfect. Practice delivering your speech to trusted members of your campaign before the event and solicit their suggestions for improvements. Check your gestures, eye contact, and expressions as well as your words. Record yourself with an audio or video recorder, listen to how you sound, and observe how you look. As you make improvements, write down what you are changing so that you remember to do it every time.

Developing a Get-Out-the-Vote Plan

All the message development and voter contact activities of your campaign will not matter if your supporters fail to vote. This is why you should begin implementing your get-out-the-vote (GOTV) plan weeks before Election Day. Your list of GOTV strategies should include voter registration and absentee ballot drives, multifaceted voter contact and mobilization operations, and Election Day hoopla and services.

Registering Voters

Supporters who are not registered cannot vote and thus cannot help you win. Those who are not registered at their current address may have difficulty voting. If you have a large constituency of potentially unregistered voters, make voter registration a priority of the campaign. At the very least, you should always have voter registration forms on hand, include a link to voter registration information on your Web site, and ask your supporters if they have registered at their current address.

You can coordinate voter registration drives with other candidates or set up a table to register voters at your events. You must keep these activities separate from your campaign activities, however, as voter registration must be nonpartisan. By setting up voter registration drives, you will benefit from identifying supportive constituencies that might not be registered, and you will be doing a service to democracy in the process.

Mobilizing Early Voters

Many voters send their ballots in early using the absentee ballot program. This means that you can get-out-the-vote before Election Day and offer an alternative to people who have difficulty making it to the polls.

Here are some ways to mobilize absentee voters:

- Track the number of absentee ballot requests in your race to determine how much of a priority it should be. If absentee voting is high in your district or jurisdiction, set up a get-out-the-vote-by-mail phone bank several weeks before the election.

- Always mention the possibility of voting by mail to supporters, especially those who do not seem sure to show up on Election Day. Send those who are interested an absentee ballot application in the mail. Make a follow-up call to confirm that they received the application from you. Call again to make sure they completed the absentee ballot application and mailed it in.

- Include the procedures for requesting an absentee ballot on your early GOTV materials and Web site.

■ **Checklist of Elements for a GOTV Plan:**

√ Number of voters needed to win.
√ Number of voters targeted in GOTV effort.
√ GOTV strategies/ mechanisms to turn out your voters.
√ Number of volunteers you will need to implement your plan.
√ Groups that will help turn out your voters.
√ How these volunteers will be recruited.
√ The money you will spend on your GOTV efforts.
√ The materials and supplies you will need.

• Organize an early absentee ballot drive and distribute absentee ballot applications at your campaign events. Get contact information from supporters who requested an absentee ballot and call them before the election to confirm that they completed and mailed in their ballots.

• Keep track of regular absentee voters who are your supporters and contact them with get-out-the-vote-by-mail phone calls several weeks before the election: Call to see if they received their ballots, then call again to make sure they mailed them in.

Forming Your Election Day Strategy

Resources are not spent at an equal rate throughout a campaign. Large amounts of resources will always be needed in the campaign's final days, especially if you are planning a major GOTV effort. Keep close tabs on your budget and supplies to ensure that you have enough for the sprint to the finish. Consultants recommend that you budget backwards in time, assessing your need for spending on get-out-the-vote activities before allocating funds for other campaign expenses.

The success of your GOTV effort will depend on how effective your voter identification program has been. If you know the households and precincts that are likely to vote for you, you will be prepared to target your efforts on Election Day.

For this reason, a good GOTV effort does not begin on Election Day. Consultants recommend that you have your plan ready to go at least a month in advance. One person should be in charge of coordinating the GOTV effort from the beginning. Set goals for the number of voters you will need to mobilize and the number of volunteers you will need to recruit to do the mobilizing. Generate a list of volunteers to help with GOTV and develop an action timeline.

Print a new batch of signs and select locations where they can be planted on Election Day. Make sure your call center has multiple phone lines available on Election Day and line up a large brigade of volunteers for GOTV phone calls, leafleting, sign-waving, poll watching, and other Election Day services. If you have done coalition building, you will be able to rely on supportive organizations to help you mobilize voters on Election Day.

The goal is to get your supporters to the polls. Mechanisms for accomplishing this include:

- Phone banks the week before the election and on Election Day, reminding people to vote and to vote for you (provide a new script for callers).
- Literature drops and door hangers on the morning of the election.
- Door-to-door visits both the weekend prior to the election and on Election Day.
- Direct mail pieces with a reminder to vote timed to reach voters the weekend before or on Election Day.
- Sign-waving at major intersections and other attention-getting stunts on Election Day.

Tell your supporters the hours and location of their polling place in these communications and do whatever you can to make it possible for them to get out and vote. Do not worry about contacting your supporters "too often." If they have not yet voted (by absentee ballot), you should continue to remind them about Election Day.

Election Day: Helping Voters Get to the Polls

Election Day is far from a day off in the campaign. Instead, your mobilizing activity should be at its peak. Many campaigns go door-to-door in the early hours of the morning to place one final door-hanger on the doors of their supporters.

You can add a blitz of new signs near polling locations or next to major roads that lead to them. Ask some of your volunteers to do sign waving at major intersections to bring attention to and generate excitement for your candidacy. Since yard signs will be useless after the election, use the remaining signs to set up prominent displays at highly trafficked locations that will help to energize supporters and remind them to vote.

Your campaign should also offer Election Day services that you promote throughout your GOTV effort. The most common service is providing rides to polling places. This service should be mentioned on campaign materials and offered to anyone who might need it. Distribute maps and directions to polling places at your office, during your last round of door-to-door canvassing, and at your sign-waving locations. If you have the resources, offer short-term babysitting services, but make sure that you make these services available regardless of how a person intends to vote. Advertise these services widely, but make sure you can deliver them. Do not put yourself in a position where you will not be able to handle the volume of requests.

Designate volunteers to serve as poll watchers who sit next to poll workers and keep track of the names of people who vote. (This is public information and your campaign is legally entitled to it.) Have them call in the information to campaign headquarters several times throughout the day. This allows the campaign to determine who needs to be mobilized. Develop a system for quickly reporting and analyzing the information, then move all available volunteers and staff to make final get out the vote calls to those who have not voted.

■ ADVICE FROM PROFESSIONALS: "Getting Out the Vote," by Phil Paule

Congratulations! You have made it—Election Day at last. The day you thought would never come has arrived. Now what do you do?

You have run a flawless campaign. The debates went well, the campaign mail was delivered on time, and the polls show you ahead, but the truth is—none of that matters. On Election Day you have to turn a well-run campaign into votes. On election night the county clerks count votes—not well-run campaigns. Getting out the vote on Election Day is what turns great candidates into elected officials.

Elections Day is the one event in a campaign that you can count on happening. The exact date is known well in advance so there is no excuse for not being prepared.

A winning campaign needs to plan for Election Day at least six weeks in advance. An effective Get-Out-The-Vote (GOTV) plan should incorporate four elements:

- Identifying OUR voters.
- Making sure they know it is Election Day.
- Getting OUR voters to the polls.
- Checking to see if they voted.

We call this the 72-hour campaign. Elections Day does not start the morning of the election; it starts 72 hours in advance. GOTV starts the Saturday before the election and continues through the close of voting on Tuesday night.

Who are OUR voters?

In order to mobilize your voters on Election Day, you will need to identify them in advance. Over the course of the campaign, develop a list that includes the names and contact information for everyone that the campaign has identified as a supporter. Your list will be made up of volunteers, donors, supporters with lawn signs, and other voters who the campaign has identified (for example, union members, NRA members, voters the candidate met while walking neighborhoods, and political party membership).

Do they know it is Election Day?

You would be surprised how common it is for people who have donated to a campaign not to vote on Election Day. People are busy. Just because you and the media are focused on Election Day, does not mean a voter will be. The kids have a doctor's appointment, the car needs new brakes, dear old grand-dad is ill. . . . Other people's lives don't revolve around Election Day the way the lives of candidates or campaign mangers do. Be sure to contact all of your voters (by phone, mail, door hangers, and/or in person) in the 72 hours leading up to Election Day with information about the date of the election, and polling hours and locations.

How do I get them to the polls?

Election Day on a well-run campaign is an exercise in logistics. It starts before the sun is up and stops when the polls close. Different types of voters must be contacted and urged to vote in a way that fits their profile. For example, with commuters, place a flyer on the windshield of their car or on top of the newspaper in the driveway to catch them on their way to work. The flyer should tell them that today is the day and it should include a map of where they need to go to cast their ballot.

Senior citizens may need a ride to the polls. Many elections have been won because a campaign provided a van at a senior center to take voters to the polls.

You will need to take the direct approach in the form of a phone call or a knock at the door to remind voters that today is the big day.

How do I check to see if they voted?

Every good 72-hour campaign has a "poll checking" operation at the larger precincts. Poll checking is nothing more than having a campaign team member enter the polling location and check to see who has cast a ballot up to that point in time. This information is public information and very valuable. If a poll is checked in the late afternoon, the list of people who have yet to cast a ballot that day is a goldmine of information. It allows you to narrow down the list of potential voters that you will need to contact in the final hours of the campaign.

Today's technology has made "poll checking" a must. Voter rolls can be loaded onto PDA's so one can easily check the polls in the late afternoon and immediately down load that information to a phone bank where calls can be made to get those who have not yet voted to the polls.

Last-minute attacks on opponents.

Often candidates who are lagging behind in the polls are tempted to launch an attack against their opponent in the final hours of the campaign. However, the last-minute attack strategy does not work. In today's voter environment people tend not to believe a late charge of malfeasance directed at another candidate. They are likely to ask, "If such information on the candidate has been around for months or even years, why is it just now, twenty-four hours before the election, being brought to our attention?" Voters typically discount last-minute attacks, and if you launch one you risk losing more voters than you gain. Such an attack may alienate your own supporters, who will choose not to volunteer or even vote for you. Last-minute attacks are not a winning campaign strategy and should be avoided.

Planning the victory party.

The victory party should always be the last thing planned by a campaign and should only be planned by people who are not part of the "ground team" on Election Day.

Many elections have been lost due to too much time spent on planning the victory celebration. This is not to say that victory celebrations are not important, but they should not be planned by the 72-hour team.

Whom to invite to the victory party is another important consideration. The party should include donors and volunteers—both have helped make the candidate's victory possible. Donors should be invited a week in advance; volunteers should pick up their tickets to the victory party at 8 p.m. after the polls have closed. They should only get a ticket when they have completed their GOTV duties.

Elections are about getting enough votes so that your candidate can go from being a candidate to a policymaker. A well-planned and equally well-executed GOTV plan is crucial to achieving this goal.

Phil Paule is a political consultant who specializes in the "Ground Game."

Last-Minute Advertising

Your advertising is an effective way to convince voters to support you, but it is no substitute for your GOTV efforts. Last-minute advertising is too late to introduce new issues or implement new tactics and it can sometimes jeopardize a campaign's momentum if it has the appearance of sleaze.

You should certainly keep up and even intensify your advertising and voter contact programs as you near the election. There is also no harm in continuing to point out differences between you and your opponent(s) on

■ **WHAT DO VOTERS WANT?**
Truthful, Relevant, and Fair Ads

Dissatisfaction with political ads was one of the first and most frequent complaints about political campaigns that focus group participants made. Participants articulated a commonly shared perception that ads function as tools of negative campaigning, which are intended to manipulate rather than inform the voter. At best, participants believe candidates use ads to publicize mostly negative and irrelevant information about their opponents. At worst, they think candidates use them to launch personal attacks, disseminate misleading information, and avoid addressing the issues that matter most to voters.

Voters want truthful, relevant, and fair ads, not "mudslinging," and they are likely to interpret attack ads launched by a candidate during the final hours of a campaign as an attempt to manipulate the voters.

legitimate grounds. Voters expect and are accepting of these types of comparative messages; however, they are not as open to last-minute attacks. For last-minute advertising to work, it must emphasize issues that the voters are already primed to hear. Candidates who believe they can turn an election by releasing or leaking new negative information about their opponent(s) risk angering and alienating voters and losing their support.

Because some candidates will resort to last-minute attacks, it is important to protect yourself against them. Have spokespeople on call to answer accusations and make sure you are accessible to the media. If your opponent(s) engage in shady tactics, point this out.

Rather than focusing on their negative tactics, bring the message back to your own positive themes. Tell the voters that your opponent(s) are trying to move the debate away from your key themes because they know how well they are resonating with voters. If you stay clean and lead by example, the contrast will show through.

Planning Your Celebration and Thanking Your Volunteers

It would be a shame to win an election and not celebrate the victory and thank everyone who was involved. Even candidates who don't win still need to thank their volunteers for their time and effort, especially if they plan to run again. Assign responsibility for planning the victory celebration to a member of your campaign who will not be directly involved in your GOTV operation. This person should reserve a space that is large enough to accommodate your volunteers, donors, and closest supporters, order refreshments, provide a sound system, and make sure that invitations go out to everyone who needs one, including members of the news media.

You should always be prepared to give a victory speech that acknowledges the contributions of your volunteers and campaign staff, is respectful of your fellow candidate(s), and then moves the conversation to governance and what you hope to accomplish in the future. No matter how much you are sure that you will win, prepare remarks congratulating your opponent(s) in case the vote does not go your way.

Conclusion: Five Things to Know about Contacting and Mobilizing Voters

1. Personal contact is key in local elections.

In local elections, the degree to which you are able to communicate your message directly to voters will play an important role in the success of your campaign. This is why having an effective field organization is so important. Personal contact enables the campaign to assess whether its messages are resonating with voters, and it gives voters a chance to be heard.

■ **BEST PRACTICE: Avoid last-minute attacks.**

They can backfire and ruin the momentum of your campaign.

2. Identify and target your audience.

Make efficient use of resources by identifying likely voters who can be convinced to support you. Target geographically by neighborhood and politically by partisan affiliation and voting pattern. You may want to cultivate relationships with particular ethnic, religious, or economic communities.

3. Combine door-to-door canvassing with phone banks.

Different people respond to different styles of mobilization. Regular phone calls can be used to identify your voters, get your message out quickly, and provide a follow-up to direct mail or canvassing. Precinct walking introduces you directly to voters, demonstrates that you are willing to work hard for their votes, and gives voters a chance to size you up.

4. Practice speaking to undecided voters.

Public speaking can be challenging, especially given the different kinds of audiences you will need to speak to in a campaign. Practice enough so that you feel comfortable and are able to get your message across while remaining responsive to the concerns of voters.

5. Develop a full-fledged GOTV operation.

To get out your vote successfully, make it a priority. Include voter registration, absentee voter mobilization, and coordinated phone, door-to-door, and mail reminders to vote. Offer Election Day services and generate excitement that will bring your voters to the polls.

Complying with the Law

8

149

It is a noble thing to run for public office—society benefits when committed and capable people use their talents to help make government work better. But a run for public office requires a commitment to learn and follow the rules governing candidates. Although the rules can sometimes seem confusing or scary, thousands of people run for office every year without violating them—and you can too!

The Two Tracks of Candidacy Regulations

To run for state or local office in California, you will need to learn and follow two different sets of rules. The first set governs your *candidacy papers*, which are the basic documents that you must file to register as a candidate for office. The second set governs *campaign finance*, which is the raising and spending of money on your candidacy. Both sets of rules have strict deadlines that require your attention. Below we describe the basic documents for each; but first, a few clarifications are in order:

> ■ **TAKE NOTE: Pay careful attention to deadlines.**
>
> Each of the candidacy documents discussed below has a specific deadline for filing. If you fail to file your declaration of candidacy and nomination petitions by the deadline — even if you are only 30 minutes late — the elections official cannot allow your candidacy without a court order. The first thing you should get from your elections official is a calendar of filing deadlines for the office you seek. We cannot stress enough the importance of filing your candidacy papers on time.

In the descriptions below, the terms "elections official" and "elections office" refer to the local office where you will receive and file your candidacy papers. It may be called the Elections Department, the Registrar's Office, or the Clerk's Office, depending on your locality. We also refer to the "FPPC," which is the state Fair Political Practices Commission, the agency charged with implementing and enforcing the campaign finance and conflicts of interest laws. Finally, we refer to the California Secretary

This chapter was written by Karen Getman, of counsel to Remcho, Johansen & Purcell and former chairman of California's Fair Political Practices Commission. Although this chapter provides an overview of the relevant law, it is not intended to be legal advice, and it cannot substitute for legal counsel.

of State, which is the office of the elected official charged with statewide implementation and monitoring of California's election laws. You likely will come in contact with all three of these entities during your candidacy.

Filing Your Candidacy Papers (On Time!)

Before you start, make sure you are currently registered to vote in the jurisdiction where you intend to run for office. That is a requirement of every candidate. If you are running for an office where you will be the nominee of a political party (as opposed to running for a nonpartisan office, like school board) make sure you have been registered with that political party for the required time period.

Everyone who runs for office in California, whether for school board or governor, has to file certain basic candidacy papers. The particulars of which documents you file, when you file them and where can differ depending on the office you are seeking.[1]

For each election, there will be a period of time—generally between 88 and 113 days out from the election—known as the *Nomination Period*.[2] During the Nomination Period, you can go to your local elections office and pick up a set of *Nominating Papers*, which are the basic candidacy documents. These will include at least[3] the following:

---

[1] This chapter does not discuss the steps that must be taken to become a write-in candidate. Not every jurisdiction allows write-in candidates, but many do. The rules and deadlines for write-in candidates can be very different from those for regular candidates. If you are considering becoming a write-in candidate, check with your local elections official.

[2] Some jurisdictions call this by other names—for example, the city of Los Angeles has a "candidate filing week" during which candidates are required to file their Declaration of Candidacy and other documents.

[3] There may be other papers as well, depending on the jurisdiction. For example, San Francisco city candidates will receive a "Declaration of Candidate Name in Chinese Characters" and the "Code of Fair Campaign Practices." Los Angeles city candidates will receive a "Statement of City-Related Business" and papers relating to the Public Matching Funds Program. *Make sure you go through all the papers you receive with a knowledgeable person at the elections office to be sure you have everything that is required.*

- **Declaration of Candidacy & Oath of Office**
- **Declaration of Filing Under Legal Name**
- **Statement of Economic Interests (FPPC Form 700)**
- **Nomination Petition & Appointment of Circulators**
- **Signature In-Lieu Petitions & Appointment of Circulators**

In addition, you may be allowed to submit a ballot statement that will appear in the voter's pamphlet.

Declaration of Candidacy & Oath of Office

The universal document that all candidates file to announce their intention to run for office is the Declaration of Candidacy & Oath of Office. You must pick up this form personally at the elections office, or designate in writing someone who is authorized to do so on your behalf. You fill out and file this form during the specified time period at the elections office; if you fill out the form outside the office, you will need a notary public to verify your signature. *You will not be allowed to file the Declaration of Candidacy past the deadline, unless you get a court order allowing the late filing—an unlikely and expensive proposition.*

Declaration of Filing Under Legal Name

The way your name appears on the Declaration of Candidacy is the way it will appear on the ballot. You are required to use your legal name, and to file a Declaration of Filing Under Legal Name. You can use a nickname if your given name or initials are shown. You also can use a shortened familiar form, such as Kate instead of Katherine. Listing your middle name is optional. You cannot use a title, such as Mr., Dr., or Rev.

Statement of Economic Interests (FPPC Form 700)

In addition to filing the Declaration of Candidacy, you also must file a candidate Statement of Economic Interests (FPPC Form 700) no later than the last day on which you could file the Declaration of Candidacy. On the Form 700 you will have to disclose certain financial interests and investments as of the date you declare your candidacy, as well as sources of income and gifts during the 12 months before filing the form. Detailed instructions are included with the form; in addition, you can ask for help from the FPPC's toll-free hotline, 1-888-ASK-FPPC.

● Nomination Petition & Appointment of Circulators

Once you have completed and turned in the Declaration of Candidacy, you will receive a set of Nomination Petitions. To qualify for the ballot, you must obtain a required number of signatures—the number varies by office—from qualified, registered voters who nominate you to run for office. Generally, only persons currently registered to vote in the jurisdiction in which you are running are qualified to sign the Nomination Petitions, and only registered voters in the jurisdiction can help circulate the Nomination Petitions on your behalf. The circulator (including you, if you collect all the signatures yourself) will sign the Affidavit of Circulator on each petition.

This probably sounds like a very easy requirement. It is not. In fact, even experienced candidates have found themselves without a sufficient number of signatures on their nomination petitions. Many people forget to re-register when they move or change names, making their registration invalid. Sometimes people who registered years ago, but failed to vote in a number of elections, are dropped from the lists of registered voters.

> ■ **TAKE NOTE: Gather extra signatures and file early.**
>
> It is common for elections officials to disqualify some signatures on the Nomination Petitions because they are from persons not registered to vote in the jurisdiction, or have some other defect. **You cannot file the Nomination Petitions later than the deadline without a court order.** Therefore, it is wise to file early and collect the maximum number of signatures allowed—well above the minimum. That way, if the elections official disqualifies some signatures, you have extras and still have time to collect even more. Some elections officials even let you check the validity of the signatures yourself, before turning in the petitions.

● Signature In-Lieu Petitions & Appointment of Circulators

In addition to turning in your Nomination Petitions, you likely will have to pay a candidate filing fee. The amount of the fee varies; for example, it costs $500 to run for a seat on the Board of Education in San Francisco, and $990 to run for a state senate or assembly seat. You can reduce or even eliminate the filing fee by turning in Signatures In Lieu of the Filing Fee. Each signature is worth a certain amount toward the filing fee (for example, 50 cents).

To do this, request in-lieu petitions from the elections official and circulate them during the allowable time period (generally starting well in advance of the deadline for Nomination Petitions). As with the signa-

> ■ **BRIGHT IDEA: Return your nomination papers early and in person.**
>
> _____
>
> That way, elections officials can notify you on the spot if something seems incomplete or incorrect on its face. If you need to re-do something, you'll have time before the deadline.

tures on the Nomination Petitions, those who sign your in-lieu petitions must be registered to vote in your jurisdiction, and those who help you circulate the petitions must be registered voters of the jurisdiction. In addition, each signer must not have signed an in-lieu petition for any other candidate running for that same office.

Signatures that you collect on your in-lieu petitions can also count as signatures for your nomination petitions, if you have collected at least twenty valid in-lieu signatures. Ask your elections official how to designate those signatures from the in-lieu petitions that you want to have counted for your nomination petitions.

• Ballot Statement

Although the documents discussed above are the basic and essential candidacy papers, there may be additional filings related to your candidacy. One of the most common is the candidate qualification statement or ballot statement. Many local jurisdictions publish a statement from each candidate in the voter's pamphlet; these are extremely useful as they may be the only thing some voters read about you! Sometimes the candidate statement is accompanied by a photograph.

State candidates get a ballot statement if they agree to abide by the voluntary expenditure limits. Make sure you find out from your local elections official, or from the Secretary of State if you are running for state office, the deadlines, length and content requirements, etc. for the candidate statement. Here again, complying with the deadline is critical. A late-filed candidate statement will not be printed in the voter's pamphlet without a court order.

Raising and Spending Money

If you are going to raise or spend $1,000 or more on your campaign, you will qualify as a "campaign committee" under state law. A candidate who will meet the $1,000 threshold must set up a bank account that will be used solely for campaign receipts and expenditures and must register a campaign committee to report all the money he or she raises and spends on the campaign. Even candidates who will not meet the $1,000 threshold have some filing obligations under the campaign finance laws. Below we review the basic steps all candidates must follow to comply with the campaign finance rules. In doing so, we discuss the following forms:

- FPPC Form 501, Candidate Intention Statement
- FPPC Form 470, Short Form Campaign Statement
- FPPC Form 410, Statement of Organization
- FPPC Form 460, Recipient Committee Campaign Statement

- FPPC Form 501 – Candidate Intention Statement

The first step for all candidates, regardless of whether they will meet the $1,000 threshold, is filing the Candidate Intention Statement – FPPC Form 501.

> ■ **TAKE NOTE: Check to see that you haven't missed anything.**
>
> Some candidates will have additional filing requirements—for instance, candidates who run in a jurisdiction with public financing, and candidates for state office who accept the voluntary spending limits. Be sure to check with someone knowledgeable—your local elections official or the FPPC—to see if you have additional requirements. You can get all the forms listed above from your local elections official; from the Secretary of State or the FPPC offices in Sacramento; or on-line at **www.fppc.ca.gov** under the "Forms" heading.

This must be done *before you solicit, raise, or spend any money on your campaign, including your own personal funds.* Form 501 is filed with the same elections official with whom you file your candidacy papers, except candidates for superior court judge file their Form 501 with the Secretary of State. It asks for basic information, such as your name, the office you are seeking, etc. If you are running for state office, Form 501 is where you indicate whether you agree to abide by the voluntary expenditure limits.[4]

---

[4] State candidates (for example, candidates for state assembly) who agree to abide by the voluntary expenditure limits are allowed to have a candidate statement published in the state voter's pamphlet. There are laws governing whether, when, and under what circumstances you can change your mind. Get advice *before* you decide whether to accept the voluntary expenditure limits.

Setting up a Campaign Bank Account

Only those candidates who will accept campaign contributions, or who will spend $1,000 or more on their campaign, must open a *separate campaign bank account*. For those candidates, however, opening the separate bank account is mandatory. The account may be opened at any state or federal bank, savings and loan association, or credit union, so long as the financial institution is located in California. You cannot have more than one bank account for each elective office you hold or seek. Most importantly, *you cannot commingle personal funds and campaign contributions*. Use the campaign bank account for all campaign contributions and expenditures, but not for anything else.

Campaign Cash, Checks, and Credit Cards

All money—including personal funds you use for the campaign—must be deposited in the campaign bank account and withdrawn as needed to pay campaign expenses. This includes "petty cash" funds. The only exception is for personal funds spent on candidate filing fees and the fees for the statement of qualifications in the ballot pamphlet. This is a rigid rule, but it serves a useful purpose in helping ensure candidates fully and accurately report all campaign contributions and expenditures. You can have a campaign credit card paid for out of the campaign bank account. This can be an existing credit card only if it has a zero balance. Again, use that credit card only for campaign expenditures, and never for your personal or business expenses.

■ **TAKE NOTE: Do not mix campaign funds and personal funds.**

Never use your personal bank account to deposit campaign contributions; they can only be deposited in a separate campaign bank account. Never use your personal bank account to make campaign expenditures unless (1) you will not meet the $1,000 threshold discussed above, or (2) the expenditures are of a type for which there is an exception.

There are rules concerning the use of cash in candidate campaigns. Generally speaking, you cannot accept a cash contribution of $100 or more; such contributions must be made by check, drawn from the contributor's account, and with the contributor's name printed on the check. You can have a petty cash fund for the campaign of no more than $100, which must come from funds that first were deposited in your campaign bank account, and then withdrawn. Only expenditures below $100 may be made with cash.

If you intend to raise or spend less than $1,000 on your campaign, the only other campaign finance document you will file is the *FPPC Form 470 – Short Form Campaign Statement* (required of all candidates who do not set up a campaign committee). If you will be raising or spending $1,000 or more, you will file the *FPPC Form 410 – Statement of Organization* and *FPPC Form 460 – Recipient Committee Campaign Statement*. All of these forms are discussed in more detail below.

■ **TAKE NOTE: Get the FPPC forms you need online.**

Remember, this guide is intended to help you learn only the basic requirements of the campaign finance laws. The FPPC publishes a lengthy and detailed manual for local candidates, and a separate one for state candidates, that discuss these various legal requirements at length and give step by step instructions on how to fill out the forms, where and when to file them, etc. Those manuals are available on the FPPC website, **www.fppc.ca.gov**, under the "Candidates" or "Publications" sections. Look for the documents entitled "Campaign Disclosure Manual 1" [for state candidates] and "Campaign Disclosure Manual 2" [for local candidates].

● FPPC Form 470 – Short Form Campaign Statement

For those candidates who will not meet the $1,000 threshold, the basic campaign finance filing is Form 470 – Short Form. In it you will verify, under penalty of perjury, that you do not intend to meet the $1,000 threshold. Filing deadlines for candidates in an election year depend on whether the election occurs in the first or second six months of the year. If it is in the first six months, then you file Form 470 either at the same time you file your declaration of candidacy, or no later than the filing deadline for the first preelection campaign committee statements (ask your elections official for that date). If your election is in the latter six months of the year, and you have received contributions or made expenditures prior to June 30 (other than expenditures for filing fees or ballot statements) then you file no later than July 31. If you did not receive contributions or make expenditures prior to June 30, then you file either with your declaration of candidacy, or no later than the filing deadline for the first preelection campaign committee statements.

Where do you file the Form 470? Candidates for superior court judge file the original and one copy with the Secretary of State, and two copies with the local elections official. Candidates for multi-county office file the original and one copy with the county elections official in the county with the most registered voters in the jurisdiction, and two copies with the elections official in the county where they live. Candidates for single-county office file the original and one copy with their county elections official, and two copies with the elections official in their home county. City candidates file the original and one copy with their local elections official.

■ TAKE NOTE: If your situation changes . . .

What if you file the Form 470, but subsequently go over the $1,000 threshold? File a **Form 470 Supplement** (or similar written notice) within 48 hours of receiving or spending $1,000. You file the Supplement with the Secretary of State; with each candidate running against you; and with your local elections official. File by fax, personal delivery, telegram, or guaranteed overnight delivery. In addition, you'll have to file the Form 410 within 10 days (or within 24 hours, if this is the final 16 days prior to your election) and you'll eventually have to file a Form 460—see below.

■ TAKE NOTE: Unsure of your filing date?

Ask your local elections official, or call the FPPC's toll free helpline, 1-866-ASK-FPPC.

• FPPC Form 410 – Statement of Organization

Any candidate who raises or spends $1,000 or more on his or her campaign must file FPPC Form 410 – Statement of Organization. This document lists the name and address of your committee, and the name of its treasurer. File the original Form 410 with the Secretary of State's office *and* file a copy with your local elections official. It must be filed within 10 days of receiving or spending $1,000—*but* if you meet the $1,000 threshold during the last 16 days before the election, you must file the Form 410 within 24 hours! You can file the Form 410 earlier, and amend it afterwards to indicate the date on which you met the $1,000 threshold. Amendments are required within 10 days of any change—for example, a change in the committee's name, or in its treasurer—*except* that if the change occurs within the last 16 days before the election, the amendment must be filed within 24 hours.

Every Campaign Committee Must Have a Treasurer

Form 410 asks for the name of your campaign treasurer. Every campaign committee must have a treasurer, and the committee may not accept contributions or make expenditures before a treasurer is appointed or while the position is vacant. Anyone can serve as treasurer, and the candidate can even be his or her own treasurer. You may, but are not required to, have an assistant treasurer. You and your treasurer will have to sign verifications on most of the major campaign finance forms, and you both are legally responsible for accurate, complete, and timely filings. The treasurer also is responsible for ensuring that the campaign meets the recordkeeping requirements of the law.

Insist that your campaign treasurer know or learn the rules for campaign accounting. Many first-time candidates use volunteers as their campaign treasurers. It's not like balancing your checkbook, however; there are special accounting rules that apply to campaigns. You wouldn't let your Aunt Ida file your business tax returns without prior experience; so don't let her file your campaign reports without becoming familiar with the reporting laws.

It is your responsibility as a candidate to make sure that the person serving as your treasurer reads the FPPC's Campaign Disclosure Manual and if possible attends an FPPC training seminar, or one put on by your local elections office. If your campaign will raise or spend a good deal of money, consider hiring a professional campaign treasurer. This is particularly important if you are a state candidate who will raise or spend $50,000 or more, because you then have an obligation to file your campaign reports electronically.

> ■ **TAKE NOTE: Form 410 as The Terminator**
>
> Form 410 is also used to terminate a committee if you lose the election, or leave office; you simply check the "termination" box at the top. However, it is important not to terminate your committee too soon. Candidates who fail in their run for office often want to close their accounts quickly and put the experience behind them. But a certain percentage of local campaign committees are subject to random audit by the FPPC every year, and the audit results may require amendment of your campaign reports. Even more likely, there may be a bill you forgot to pay, or a refund due you—many cities and counties make a partial refund of the candidate filing fee, for example, but not until weeks after the election. If this happens and you have already closed your campaign bank account, these small items can become a big headache!

Keeping Accurate Records

Recordkeeping is an essential aspect of running a good campaign. All campaign committees are subject to audit by the state Franchise Tax Board, and by the FPPC. State law requires that candidates keep accurate records, including original source documents, for four years from the date of filing the campaign statement to which the records are tied. (If you receive contributions from "affiliated entities," the documents must be kept for five years.) The bank statements, cancelled checks, check registers, and credit card statements can serve as a "daily record" of expenditures.

For all expenditures of $25 or more, you must have a record of the full name and address of the recipient, the date of the expenditure and/or the date the goods were received, and a description of what was bought. All contributions of $25 or more must be documented with the name and address of the contributor and the date you received the contribution. Make a copy of any contribution check before you deposit it. Once someone has contributed a cumulative total of $100 or more during a calendar year to your campaign, you must document the contributor's occupation and employer. *A contribution of $100 or more must be returned if, within 60 days of receipt, you do not have the contributor's name, address, occupation and employer.*

• FPPC Form 460 – Recipient Committee Campaign Statement

If you raise or spend $1,000 or more on your campaign, you meet the threshold for becoming a candidate committee. Once you do, you will have to file FPPC Form 460 – Recipient Committee Campaign Statement. This is the basic campaign finance disclosure form filed by most candidate committees in California, from Governor down to school board member.

On this form you will record all campaign contributions, including the name, address, occupation and employer, and cumulative contributions of the contributor; all campaign expenditures, including the name and address of the vendor and any subvendors associated with the expenditure; accrued expenses, that is, money that you know you owe but have not yet paid; outstanding loans made or received; and any other miscellaneous increases or decreases to your campaign account.

The Form 460 is filed in the same places as the Form 470, described in detail above. When to file the Form 460 is a more complicated question, however. The filing deadlines are keyed to the dates of the particular election and the office for which you are running. Ask your elections official for a calendar of filing dates. You also can find a calendar on the FPPC website, under the "When to File" section of the Candidate listings.

Detailed instructions on how to fill out Form 460 and its many schedules, are provided with the form and in the FPPC Campaign Disclosure Manual.

Form 460 is a little like the IRS income tax forms—it has its own terminology and ways of recording information that are not always intuitive. Even the most knowledgeable and experienced professional treasurers have to ask the FPPC for help in filling out the Form 460 correctly.

Part of the difficulty stems from the complex and detailed nature of the state campaign finance rules. When you are filling out Form 460, you will be accounting for every dollar that is associated with your campaign, and there is a rule governing how each of those dollars must be accounted for. This chapter cannot possibly teach you all the rules. What we will try to do instead is alert you to some of the commonly misunderstood or misapplied rules. That is no substitute, however, for acquiring a basic understanding of the campaign finance reporting rules. *If you intend to raise or spend any significant sum of money on your campaign, read through the FPPC Campaign Disclosure Manual and, if possible, attend a new candidate training seminar.* The time you spend doing these things up front can save you thousands of dollars in fines later on!

> ■ **TIP FROM THE PROS**
>
> You or your treasurer must read the Form 460 instructions and the FPPC Campaign Disclosure Manual; don't think you can fill out the form correctly without doing so! There is no substitute for acquiring a basic understanding of the campaign finance reporting rules. If possible, attend a new candidate training seminar.

Basic Rules to Follow

There are certain basic rules that everyone in your campaign, including you, should memorize:

- No cash contributions or expenditures of $100 or more.
- No anonymous contributions of $100 or more; no money orders or cashier's checks; no contributions from non-U.S. citizens.
- Keep track of the name, address, occupation, and employer of all donors who

contribute $25 or more. (You'll have to return contributions of $100 or more for which you don't have the required information.)
- Keep copies of all contribution checks and all expenditure receipts and checks.
- Don't use campaign funds for personal expenses.
- Always disclose the true source of a campaign contribution and any intermediary to the transaction.

If you are subject to contribution limits, you must make sure that the cumulative contributions of each donor do not exceed the limit for that election. And remember that your local jurisdiction may have different, even stricter rules, than the state.

Events that Trigger Special, More Complicated Requirements

In addition to knowing the basic rules, make sure you and your campaign treasurer understand what types of events trigger more complicated rules. If one of those events seems likely to occur, get help from legal counsel or someone else familiar with campaign law.

The most common events that trigger special rules are:

- Mailing more than 200 pieces of campaign literature.
- Sending a written solicitation for campaign contributions.
- Having a fundraiser at someone's home.
- Receiving $5,000 or more from a single contributor.
- Receiving $1,000 or more from a single contributor in the last sixteen days prior to the election.
- In-kind contributions (for example, volunteer personal services, free printing, etc.). How to value these can be tricky.
- Payments made by someone to vendors on your behalf.
- Using campaign money for tickets, automobile expenses, or clothing.
- Getting a loan for your campaign; making a loan to your campaign.
- Getting a discount on goods or services.

Be aware that if one of these common events occurs, you will have to know and comply with the particular rule governing it.

Other Prohibitions and Forms

This chapter does not discuss every prohibition concerning campaign contributions and expenditures that may apply to your candidacy. The prohibitions are set out in the FPPC's information manuals. Become aware of these prohibitions before you start fundraising for your campaign!

Also, the forms discussed above are not the only forms that may apply to your campaign. Here are a few others of which you should be aware:

■ **TAKE NOTE: Be especially vigilant with late contribution reports.**

Because late contributions can help turn the tide in an election, the public must be notified of them immediately. During the last 16 days before an election, you must file a special report **within 24 hours** of receiving $1,000 or more from a single source. The report should be filed on **FPPC Form 497 – Late Contribution Report**, available from your local elections official or from the websites of the FPPC and the Secretary of State. The FPPC reacts very harshly to candidates, even first-time candidates, who fail to file late contribution reports on time.

- FPPC Form 495 – Supplemental Preelection Campaign Statement—used in certain circumstances if your committee makes contributions totaling $10,000 or more to other candidates or ballot measures.

- FPPC Form 511 – Paid Spokesperson Report—used when a committee spends $5,000 or more for an individual's appearance in an advertisement or telephone message to support or oppose a ballot measure.

- Special Odd-Year Report—A Form 460 that is filed on a special timeline during odd-numbered years if the committee makes contributions of $10,000 or more to state candidates or to committees primarily formed to support or oppose state candidates.

- FPPC Form E-530—Filed only by committees that are required to file electronically with the Secretary of State, and used to disclose expenditures of

$50,000 or more for a communication made within forty-five days of an election that clearly identifies a state candidate.

Getting More Help

It is daunting to realize what it takes to ensure your campaign complies with its legal filing requirements. If you plan to raise or spend a significant sum of money, or face strong opposition, you should think about hiring a professional campaign manager, who can help you decide whether you also need a professional treasurer and/or a campaign lawyer. *There are a few situations when getting good legal help is essential*:

1. If you miss a deadline for filing one of your candidacy papers.

2. If your campaign has committed a violation of the campaign reporting laws, or you suspect that it might have done so, even inadvertently.

No matter what the situation, however, the most important thing you can do is *ask for help before you take action*. A few words of cautionary advice can make all the difference to your campaign.

Conclusion: Five Things to Know about Complying with the Law

1. Follow both sets of rules.
Two sets of rules govern elections for state and local office in California. One set regulates your candidacy papers, the other set regulates your campaign finance. Become familiar with both sets of rules along with the forms and filing deadlines associated with them.

2. File your candidacy papers on time.
Don't risk being precluded from running for office because you did not file your candidacy papers on time. Deadlines may vary by locality and the office you are seeking. Ask your elections officer for a calendar of filing deadlines. Gather the maximum (rather than minimum) number

of signatures required for your Nominating Petitions to ensure that you will have enough valid signatures to qualify for the ballot. Turn those signatures in early.

3. Make sure everyone who works on your campaign knows and complies with the law.

Campaign laws govern not only the candidate, but everyone who works on a candidate's campaign. Make sure that your staff and volunteers are aware of and follow the basic rules that govern raising and spending campaign money. Don't risk you or a member of your staff making a mistake that will sink your candidacy.

4. Seek out more information.

This chapter provides only a basic overview of the rules governing state and local elections. Depending upon your locality and the type of office you are seeking, there may be other forms and prohibitions that are not covered in the pages above. Seek out more information from the links provided in this chapter to ensure that you are fully versed in the rules governing your election.

5. Ask for help.

Many of these laws are complicated and difficult to comprehend. Ask a knowledgeable person at your local elections office to walk you through the required paperwork. Get legal help if you miss a deadline for filing one of your candidacy papers or if you think your campaign may have committed a violation of the campaign reporting laws.

Conclusion: Winning the Right Way

9

From precampaign planning to Election Day GOTV drives, we have provided you with an overview of how to build your campaign for public office. This book gives you the tools and advice you need to begin planning, organizing, fundraising, and developing and delivering your message to voters. Now you are ready to begin the hard work of campaigning.

Key Points to Review before You Start:

- Well before the campaign begins, learn more about the concerns of your community and the demands of public office and successful campaigning. There are many ways to get involved in local politics and local issues before your campaign kicks off—and every effort you make will pay off once the campaign begins.

- Plan your campaign from the beginning, rather than make ad hoc decisions as they arise. Build a winning strategy, complete with a budget and a timeline, and then devote your energies to implementing it.

- Build a competent and motivated organization of paid staff and volunteers. Choose your key staff members and divide responsibilities among them. Identify, recruit, and use a large base of volunteers, and build coalitions with local organizations.

- Develop a compelling and consistent message for your campaign. Give voters a reason to vote for you by articulating your rationale, theme, and issue positions. Select the issues that you will focus on carefully and find a way to differentiate yourself from your fellow candidate(s) without succumbing to attack politics.

- Raise the resources needed to get your message out to voters. Develop a fundraising plan, identify small and large potential donors, and get comfortable asking for money. Use fundraising letters and events to increase your pool of resources.

- Deliver your message to voters. Inform voters using earned media, advertising, and public events. Make your campaign accessible to the media and communicate effectively with reporters. Make debates and interactive public forums central to your efforts. Use an effective combination of advertising, which includes direct mail, signs and written materials, the Web and email, and electronic media.

- Make direct contact with and mobilize as many voters as you can. Identify your target audience of undecided voters and use phone and door-to-door canvassing to convince them to support your candidacy. Energize your supporters and make sure they get to the polls on Election Day.

- Comply with all campaign laws. Pay attention to the legal requirements that you must follow to be an official candidate. Comply with all deadlines and obligations associated with being an official candidate and follow all campaign finance regulations.

Making Sense of All the Advice

In addition to the overview that we have provided, you have read the recommendations of professional political consultants, who are specialists in every major area of campaigning. You have read the advice of those who have been on the "front lines" of campaigning. You even have read about what voters want from campaigns, based on research we and others have collected using public opinion polls and focus groups.

Now it is time for you to develop your own perspective on campaigning by synthesizing these diverse insights and integrating them with your own experiences. As you proceed with your campaign and consider what advice to incorporate and what to leave out, keep in mind that most campaign experts and practitioners agree on a few key points:

- You can win public office by running an ethical and effective campaign. You do not have to sacrifice your principles to win. You only have to commit yourself to working hard, following the rules, and taking your obligations as a candidate seriously.

- Successful campaigns are well planned. Think through your message development, organization, fundraising, and message delivery strategies before you begin. Make decisions based on a clear plan of action to achieve your goals, rather than the considerations of the moment.

- Voters will never be as attentive to your campaign as you would like them to be. You have to use your scarce time and resources to create opportunities to interact with voters. Make these interactions count by using a consistent and compelling message to convince voters to support you.

- Most campaigns need to devote significant energy to fundraising. Additional resources, whether they are spent on advertising or contacting voters, allow you to deliver your message to more voters and mobilize more supporters to vote.

- You cannot campaign alone. Successful candidates are backed by effective organizations, including full-time management and motivated volunteers.

- Different voters react to different kinds of campaign communications. Create a diverse communications strategy that includes talking to the media, being active at public events, directly contacting voters, and advertising in different venues.

Your Timeline

Campaigns require advanced planning, action taken on multiple fronts, and the smooth operation of numerous activities often simultaneously. It can be difficult to keep track of how and when to implement all of the components of a successful campaign. Here is a general campaign timeline to follow:

Months or years before the campaign:
- Learn about the people, the problems, and the controversies in your community.
- Get involved in local political and social organizations.
- Develop the expertise and experience to address local concerns.

Before you begin actively campaigning:

- Follow all the rules to ensure your name is on the ballot.
- Develop a plan that addresses all aspects of your campaign; it should include a budget, a finance plan, a media plan, a GOTV plan, and a calendar.
- Build a core organization, including a manager and a treasurer.
- Decide on a basic campaign message and practice talking to voters.
- Gather seed money to get started with your campaign.

In the first few months of your campaign:

- Kick-off your campaign with a well-publicized event.
- Speak to community groups, build coalitions, and gather endorsements.
- Develop a campaign Web site and email list.
- Create printed campaign materials that emphasize your message.
- Raise funds for your campaign by contacting potential donors with phone calls and fundraising letters.
- Hold several fundraising events and distribute your campaign materials.
- Prepare and submit your campaign finance reporting materials.
- Recruit volunteers and paid staff to expand your organization.
- Identify undecided voters and likely target constituencies.
- Decide on your advertising and voter contact strategy and develop the infrastructure to implement it.

In the middle of your campaign:

- Create and participate in public forums, including debates with other candidates and town-hall meetings on your own.
- Generate news by holding public events, issuing press releases, and giving interviews to reporters.
- Send another round of fundraising letters and call back your supporters.
- Contact undecided voters and set up regular telephone and door-to-door canvassing operations.
- Hold neighborhood events for undecided voters to get to know you, preferably in combination with your efforts to contact voters.
- Distribute signs and materials to increase your name identification.
- Increase your volunteer base and organize your GOTV efforts.

Near the end of your campaign:

- Increase your visibility by participating in public forums and media interviews as well as rallies with supporters.
- Send targeted mail and use electronic media advertising to get your message across to undecided voters.
- Make your final round of fundraising pleas using mail, phone calls, and fundraising events.
- Contact undecided voters through intensified telephone and door-to-door canvassing operations.
- Mobilize supporters with reminders about Election Day and opportunities for early voting.
- Achieve maximum publicity for your candidacy by distributing all of your yard-signs, identifying new large sign locations, and updating your old signs.
- Make regular statements and send regular press releases highlighting your campaign's progress and responding to anticipated or current attacks from your opponent(s).

At the end of your campaign:

- Launch a final round of targeted advertising to convince undecided voters.
- Target undecided voters with a final round of phone and door-to-door canvassing.
- Contact all supporters with a GOTV phone call, direct mail piece, and/or home visit. Include information on your GOTV services.
- Make immediate public statements to respond to all attacks.
- Prepare and submit final disclosure of contributions.

On Election Day:

- Leave a GOTV door-hanger at your supporters' homes.
- Use sign-waving to generate excitement.
- Implement GOTV services and monitor turnout at the polls.
- Call your supporters who have not voted.

Running for Office on the High Road

If you follow the advice in this book, you will be implementing ethical and effective strategies for winning public office. While remembering that voters care more about your substantive positions, character, and experience than the campaign tactics that you adopt, you can use your winning strategy to build a reputation as a candidate who is taking the "high road" to public service and increase your support among voters.

Make sure that the voters know about the best practices adopted by your campaign, such as your openness regarding your fundraising and your willingness to meet with voters and the press, the steps that you have taken to bring additional voters into the process, and the substantive focus of your campaign message—especially if these practices contrast with the strategies of the other candidate(s). If you emphasize only your campaign strategies, however, voters will not hear the central message of your campaign, that is, what you hope to accomplish if elected.

There are several things you can do to take advantage of your high-road strategy without distracting voters from your primary message:

- Make it clear when you announce your candidacy that you plan to run an ethical campaign and expect the same from the other candidate(s). Outline the steps you will take to increase voters' confidence in the process, for example, by disclosing the sources of your campaign funds, mobilizing new voters, and making the issues that matter to voters central to your campaign's message.

- Sign a code of conduct or make a public pledge to run an ethical campaign and challenge your opponent(s) to do the same. Ask the media and community organizations to monitor the degree to which you and your opponent(s) keep your commitments to adopt ethical campaign strategies.

- Make it known to the media, your fellow candidate(s), and undecided voters that you are willing to debate regularly, that you have planned a schedule of town-hall meetings and get-to-know-the-candidate events, and that you have answered hundreds of voter questions using email, phone, and direct contact.

- When you make comparisons or speak negatively about your opponent(s), explain why these criticisms are substantive and relevant to the office. Provide documentation of all negative claims to the media and make it available on your Web site.

- When attacks come your way, offer a clear response and back up any explanation you give with documentation. When you respond to an attack, make it clear that you are waging a different kind of campaign and say why voters should reject candidates who launch misleading, irrelevant, or unfair attacks.

- Always remember that you will find an attack on your candidacy or a questionable statement by an opponent more objectionable than the voters. It is important to establish an image as an ethical campaigner and point out clear transgressions by your opponent(s) without jeopardizing your focus on your message. If you make a point about your campaign practices, use it to transition to your qualifications and plans for government.

After You Are Elected: Succeeding in Governance

Getting elected to office is only the first challenge you will face as a public servant. Do not assume that you will know how to govern based on your campaign experience. On the other hand, do not forget what you learned once you get elected. Many of the same principles of campaigning apply to governance, but keep the similarities and the differences in mind.

Most public officials run for office more than once and your next campaign is never very far away. After the campaign is over, however, fulfilling your role as a public servant will entail many of the same practices and skills you relied upon as a candidate.

First, you will need to communicate regularly with the public and the media. Your skill at making succinct points and delivering coherent messages will come in handy when you attempt to make law or implement policy. Making yourself available to reporters and preparing for your interactions with the media should also remain a priority.

Second, just as in your campaign, you will need to rely on a broad organization, rather than doing everything yourself. Building a strong staff (if you have one) and fostering a good relationship with agency staff along with developing an organization of supporters to help you govern should remain a priority. As in campaigns, you will need to form coalitions with other organizations and elected officials.

Third, planning your strategies, budgeting carefully, and making the best use of your time and resources are all skills needed to govern effectively. Finally, you will need to maintain openness and accountability while in office. Follow all ethics rules that govern elected officials and disclose any conflicts of interest you may have. Make yourself available to constituents by holding regular town-hall meetings and by maintaining an office with a staff that is accessible and responsive to constituent concerns.

Governing is not one big campaign, however. You will need to adapt to several new realities once in office. First, accomplishing legislative or administrative initiatives often requires working across ideological lines with those who may not have supported your candidacy. Do not lose potential supporters for your efforts by holding grudges against those who were not with you on Election Day.

Second, voters expect more civility and less conflict in public office than in campaigns. They recognize that substantive comparative discussions can take place in campaigns but are more wary of open conflict once you are in office. Third, you will have to pay more attention to the details of policy and administration, including issues that will not be of concern to voters. It will also be more difficult to please everyone when you implement policy than when you make public statements about it.

Finally, it is likely that you will spend more time talking to particular stakeholders than to the public at large. While your responsibility is to a broad constituency, only a small minority will be actively involved in influencing decisions. Even so, make every effort to take a broad set of ideas and interests into consideration when making decisions.

To make your transition to governing run smoothly, the best idea is to talk to those who have held the office before you and to other elected and appointed officials who you will need to work with while in office. Even if they did not support your candidacy, try to remain open to their advice. You may want to change how the office is run, but be respectful of the person you are replacing and ask him or her to share what he or she has learned while in office. You can always choose to change directions later, but your first priority in office should be to learn how the system works.

As you enter office, do not forget about the promises you made as a candidate and the priorities that you set in the campaign. Voters will be counting on you to act on these. If you change your mind or cannot implement something you proposed, apologize and explain why. If you set goals during the campaign, regularly ask yourself if you are meeting those goals.

Problems that you did not anticipate as a candidate are likely to arise, and it is wise to change focus as events or new information necessitate. The important point is that you gain a reputation as an effective leader by setting your priorities and working toward them. Remember, your next campaign will be built upon your achievements in office.

Building a Career, Not Just a Campaign

Candidates and campaign advisors often get caught up in the excitement and the daily events of the campaign. They have their eyes on winning the election and see it as the only priority. This kind of focus is useful for winning elections as long as it is tempered by the realization that this is not your final competition, your only challenge, or an isolated event. Your campaign will likely set the stage for your career in public life.

You will be convincing voters to support your goals, mobilizing the electorate to vote for you, and planning your issue positions and strategies for more than just one campaign. You may be working with the same reporters, organizational leaders, and voters for many years. If you develop a reputation early in your career as an unethical politician who bends the rules and stretches the truth, that reputation is likely to stay with you. If you make decisions that reflect your true values with an eye toward your ethical responsibilities and long-term interests, you can build a reputation as an effective leader and a rising star in local politics.

The American public's current view of politics and politicians is quite negative. Voters are disdainful of a politician's promises and constituents rarely believe that an elected official is looking out for their interests. Politics does not have to be this way. As an aspiring participant in public life, you can choose to be part of the solution rather than part of the problem.

We commend you for taking an active role in the concerns of your community and we encourage you to work toward improving the political climate in your area by taking your campaign decisions seriously. By running an ethical and effective campaign that is open and accountable and by using your campaign to inform and mobilize voters, you can make a contribution before you are ever elected to office. Good luck in your campaign and thank you for assuming this responsibility that a democracy demands.

Contributors

Polly Armstrong is part of the third generation of community-involved women in her family. Her grandmother was a suffragette; her mother was a life-long League of Women Voters devotee; and Armstrong spent sixteen years involved in Berkeley city government. While raising two daughters with the help of her husband John, Armstrong led Campfire Girl troops; presided over PTAs; attained her Certified Financial Planning degree and started a consulting service to help women control their finances; did a stint as a "puller" on a salmon fishing boat; became a certified SCUBA diver; earned her private pilot's license; and became a breast cancer survivor. Now in retirement, Armstrong consults with a local developer, flies around the country with her husband, and finds total joy in her new granddaughter Lucy Rose.

Katie Burke is originally from Three Rivers, California, and now lives in Washington, D.C., where she works as a congressional aide for Representative Rosa DeLauro (D-Connecticut, 3rd). In 2003, Burke graduated with highest honors from the University of California, Berkeley, where she majored in political science. While at UC Berkeley, Burke worked for Loni Hancock's state assembly campaign, Tom Bates's mayoral campaign, and spent a semester in Washington as an intern for the research department of EMILY's List, a political action committee that supports the campaigns of pro-choice Democratic women.

Joanne Davis has spent the last twenty years working with top elected officials, state political parties, public opinion leaders, and corporate executives in both California and nationwide. In 2002, Davis served as Statewide Finance Director for the 2002 Bill Simon for Governor Campaign, overseeing fundraising efforts that raised over $21 million for the general election cycle. She served in the same position for the primary election campaign of Richard Riordan for Governor. In 1994 Davis served as campaign manager for the re-election of Attorney General Dan Lungren, coordinating the efforts that resulted in a landslide victory over the challenger. In 1998, she designed and implemented a comprehensive fundraising program that raised over $32 million for Lungren's gubernatorial race. As president of The Davis Group, Davis has led the fundraising efforts for many other political and nonprofit clients, including Bush for President, Victory 2000; the Assembly Republican PAC; Keith Olberg for Secretary of State; the Los Angeles World Affairs Council; the Republican National Committee; and the California Republican Party.

Mitchell Englander is Chief of Staff to Los Angeles City Councilman Greig Smith. He is also the founding principal of Issue Strategies, Inc., a public affairs, government relations, and political consulting firm in Los Angeles that services numerous political campaigns and corporate clients on government and community relations. Englander has successfully managed scores of local, state, and federal election contests, and he is a leading expert in the use of computer technology for public affairs programs, marketing strategies, coalition building, and outreach campaigns. Englander is the president and cofounder of the California chapter of the American Association of Political Consultants. He has been honored with numerous "Pollie" awards from the national chapter of the AAPC as well as awards from the International Association of Business Communicators (IABC), and the Public Relations Society of America (PRSA). He lives in Glendale, California, with his wife of ten years, Jayne Englander, and their two daughters, Lindsey and Lauren.

Karen Getman is of counsel to Remcho, Johansen & Purcell, one of the leading political, constitutional and policy law firms in California. A graduate of Yale College and Harvard Law School, she was appointed chairman of the California Fair Political Practices Commission by Governor Gray Davis in March 1999, and served in that capacity until April 2003. She has extensive experience in state and federal courts and before administrative agencies, and represents a variety of clients in public policy and constitutional litigation. She also advises public officials, candidates, committees, and public agencies on all aspects of the electoral and political process, including compliance with the state Political Reform Act and the federal Bi-Partisan Campaign Reform Act. During the 2003-2004 academic year, she served as the first Executive in Residence at the Center on Politics at the University of California, Berkeley's Institute of Governmental Studies, where she continues as a visiting scholar. She is also adjunct professor at Boalt Hall School of Law, where she co-teaches a course on regulating public integrity.

Matt Grossmann is a researcher at the Center for Campaign Leadership and a Ph.D. candidate in political science at the University of California, Berkeley. He has researched political campaigns for the California Commission on Internet Political Practices, the Center for Democracy and Technology, the Center for Voting and Democracy, and the Institute of Governmental Studies. He helped organize campaigns for local initiatives, in the British Parliament, and for U.S. legislative and municipal offices. He has worked as a volunteer organizer, a political party operative, a legislative staff member, a news reporter, and a grassroots activist. As a volunteer and staff member, Grossmann has walked precincts, served on political party boards, raised money, and organized events.

Jarryd Gonzales is the executive director of Victory 2004 for the California Republican Party. As executive director, Gonzales, on behalf of the state party, is responsible for overseeing the statewide coordinated political effort that includes the presidential, U.S. Senate and congressional campaigns. Additionally, Jarryd serves as the political director of the California Republican Party. Prior to his work at the California Republican Party, he served as a campaign manager, political director, and chief spokesperson on numerous legislative and statewide contests. In 2003, Gonzales served as an international political trainer for the International Republican Institute in Venezuela, where he trained party leaders on how to develop and execute a campaign plan. He also serves as an instructor for the Republican National Committee's 72 Hour Task Force. Gonzales is a graduate of the University of Southern California, where he earned his bachelor's degree in international relations.

Mary Hughes has provided strategic guidance to candidates for president, Congress, and state offices for over twenty years. She is a co-founder and president of Staton & Hughes, a strategic communications and political consulting firm in San Francisco, California. During the 1990s, Staton & Hughes helped convert four Republican-held California congressional seats for Democrats—Anna Eshoo, Mike Thompson, Ellen Tauscher, and Susan Davis. The firm has also directed successful campaigns for California Assembly and State Senate candidates. Hughes also directed campaigns resulting in a number of successful "firsts" in California and national politics: the first woman superintendent of schools, Delaine Eastin; the first open lesbian judge in the nation, Donna

Hitchens; and the first Latino mayor of San Jose, Ron Gonzalez. Hughes is a senior advisor to House Democratic Leader Nancy Pelosi with whom she worked on the leadership races. She received her law degree from the University of Virginia and her undergraduate degree from Mount Holyoke College.

Valerie Hyman has thirty years of experience working as a television reporter, newsroom manager, and corporate news executive. She was the founding director of the Program for Broadcast Journalists at The Poynter Institute in St. Petersburg, Florida, a nonprofit, educational organization, where she spent a decade leading seminars and conferences in management, reporting, writing, and enterprise thinking. As a reporter, Hyman was awarded the DuPont-Columbia Silver Baton, the Peabody Award, two National Headliner Awards, the Sigma Delta Chi Distinguished Service Medal, and Tennessee Broadcaster of the Year. She spent a year at Harvard as a Nieman Fellow, followed by nearly two years as director of news development for the Gillett Group of network-affiliated television stations. Now president of The Management Coach, Hyman provides coaching and consultation for networks, station groups, and their news directors; strategic planning; and workshops on writing and reporting, enterprise thinking, ethics, and newsroom management.

Shaun R. Lumachi is a dedicated leader who serves his community through advocacy and the development of relationships. Lumachi is president of Chamber Advocacy, a professional advocacy consulting firm that builds advocacy programs, which empower chamber of commerce members to leverage their voices and increase their relevance in public policy discussions and decision making. He earned a Bachelor of Arts degree in government from California State University, Sacramento. He is a resident of Long Beach, California.

Michelle Maravich is one of California's leading political fundraisers. She has designed and managed fundraising efforts for more than twenty-five candidates for public office over the past fourteen years. For the past five statewide campaign cycles, she has led the fundraising efforts for the California Democratic Party and the California Coordinated Campaign, which enabled Democrats to win statewide and legislative offices in historic margins. She directed the fundraising for the California Delegation activities for the Democratic National Committee (DNC) in Chicago 1996, Los Angeles 2000, and Boston 2004. In addition, she leads the finance team for Attorney General Bill Lockyer. She holds a B.A. degree with honors in political science from UCLA and lives in Los Angeles with her husband and son.

Phil Paule has been involved in Republican campaigns since 1988. He is known for running day-to-day "ground game" operations. He has managed campaigns from the local level to targeted congressional races. During the 1990s he served as political director for the California Republican Party. Paule is well versed in the use of voter files, coalition building, and earned media. He is the principal of Paule Consulting, Inc., and is a member of the American Association of Political Consultants. He and his wife Julie live in Temecula, California.

Dan Schnur is one of California's leading Republican political and media strategists, whose record includes work on four presidential and four gubernatorial campaigns, as well as extensive experience on behalf of a variety of nonprofit organizations and private-sector companies. Schnur served as the national director of communications for the 2000 presidential campaign of U.S. Senator John McCain. In addition, he has advised a variety of Republican candidates and causes throughout his career, including five years as chief media spokesman for California Governor Pete Wilson. Schnur is founding principal of COMMANDFOCUS, a Sacramento-based public affairs, communications, and campaign management firm, and he writes regularly for several California newspapers, including the *Los Angeles Times,* the *San Francisco Chronicle* and the *Sacramento Bee.* In addition, he acts as an analyst and political commentator for CNN, MSNBC, and Fox News. Schnur is currently a visiting instructor at UC Berkeley's Institute of Governmental Studies and an adjunct professor at the University of Southern California's Annenberg School for Communication, where he teaches courses in politics and communications.

Christine Trost is an associate specialist at the Institute of Governmental Studies and a lecturer in political science at the University of California, Berkeley. Since earning her Ph.D. in political science from UC Berkeley in 2000, Trost has led the research arm of IGS's *Improv-*

ing Campaigns Project. The project is dedicated to studying the role of political consultants in campaigns and to identifying and developing a set of best practices that can be taught to the next generation of political consultants and candidates. Trost also has experience in grassroots politics. Before entering graduate school she was a student organizer and canvass director for a public interest group in Massachusetts and Wisconsin, respectively. In 2000, she was director of the California Alliance for Better Campaigns, which was part of a nationwide alliance of public interest groups dedicated to increasing television coverage of local, state, and national political campaigns.

Bob Wickers has provided media, polling, and strategic communication services for political candidates and corporate clients throughout the United States and abroad since 1987. In 2002, Wickers provided general strategic and media services for Minnesota U.S. Senator Norm Coleman in his dramatic victory over former Vice President Walter Mondale, contributing to the Republican takeover of the United States Senate. In addition, he produced media, conducted strategic research, and helped guide the successful campaigns of Arkansas Governor Mike Huckabee, Nebraska Governor Mike Johanns, Texas Lt. Governor David Dewhurst, and Nebraska Attorney General Jon Bruning—recording a clean, five for five, sweep for his clients in 2002. In 1996 Wickers was part of the American team that guided Russian President Boris Yeltsin's successful re-election campaign. That effort earned him and his colleagues a *TIME Magazine* cover story and the International Consultant of The Year POLLIE Award presented by the American Association of Political Consultants. Wickers cofounded his firm, Dresner, Wickers & Associates, which is based in San Francisco, in 1993.

Jonathan Wilcox is a corporate communications and public affairs consultant, providing executive speechwriting and media training to clients in the public and private sectors. He is also an adjunct faculty member of the University of Southern California's Annenberg School for Communication. In 2003, he served as communications director for Rescue California, the lead committee promoting the recall of former Governor Gray Davis. Wilcox was chief deputy speechwriter for former California Governor Pete Wilson and has written for numerous corporate executives, including the chairman and CEO of Merrill Lynch, the CEO of

Coldwell Banker, and the executive vice president of Wells Fargo Bank. He has also authored remarks for Ronald Reagan and former California Governor George Deukmejian. His editorial commentaries have been featured in the *National Review, Sacramento Bee, Los Angeles Daily News, San Francisco Examiner, Washington Times, Houston Chronicle, Dallas Morning News* and *Cleveland Plain Dealer*.

Resources for Further Reading

Books & Periodicals

Beaudry, Ann, and Bob Schaffer. 1986. *Winning Local and State Elections: The Guide to Organizing Your Campaign*. New York: Free Press.

Campaigns & Elections – all issues of the magazine.

Faucheux, Ron. 2003. *Winning Elections: Political Campaign Management, Strategy & Tactics*. New York: Evans & Company.

Grey, Lawrence. 1994. *How to Win a Local Election: A Complete Step-By-Step Guide*. New York: M. Evans and Company.

Moffit, Mary Anne. 2001. *Campaign Strategies and Message Design: A Practitioner's Guide from Start to Finish*. Connecticut: Praeger.

Shea, Daniel M., and Michael John Burton. 2001. *Campaign Craft: The Strategies, Tactics, and Art of Political Campaign Management*. Connecticut: Praeger.

Web sites

California Fair Political Practices Commission (http://www.fppc.ca.gov)

Center for Campaign Leadership (http://campaigns.berkeley.edu/)

Center for Communication and Civic Engagement (http://depts.washington.edu/ccce/civicengagement/)

Institute for Local Self Government (http://www.ilsg.org)

Local Victory (http://www.localvictory.com)

Project on Campaign Conduct (http://www.campaignconduct.org)